PRAISE FOR COURAGE TO SHINE

"There is deep wisdom on every page. Sara is a spiritual and health leader for our time. Read this empowering book to design your life into greater happiness and fulfillment."

RACHAEL JAYNE GROOVER, BESTSELLING AUTHOR OF
POWERFUL AND FEMININE

"Sara Regester says she is 'inspired by stress,' and she means it! In *Courage to Shine*, we learn that stress is, indeed, an invitation to spiritual growth. Sara shares her own tender journey, loads of practical tips, and fresh ideas for deepening in our spiritual growth and enjoying greater self-mastery in our relationships, professions, and more. Read this book and thrive!"

REV. KAREN RUSSO, MBA, AUTHOR OF THE MONEY KEYS

"This book helped me recognize the patterns I'm stuck in that create stress. I learned new wisdom and tools to transform my stress into growth. I recommend this book to anyone who wants to experience freedom when you stretch outside your comfort zone."

SUSAN RAYMOND, LANDSCAPE ARCHITECT

"Thirty years of career stress, on top of the regular challenges of life, steered me to a pattern of overworking, over-giving and codependency in order to feel safe and needed. This book highlights exactly how to move out of my stale, confining and limiting comfort zone to previously unimaginable opportunities. Now, every day, I remind myself that Attention = Power and that what I focus on, I get more of. I am learning how to bring my light back to myself."

MARY, MARKET MANAGER

"If you want to live your most authentic, courageous, and purpose-driven life, *Courage to Shine* is for you. Most of us can relate to the many glimpses of how we sell ourselves, and those in our lives, short. Having lived much of my life as a perfectionist people-pleaser, I know that I do. It takes mindfulness, vulnerability, bravery, and practice to step into both the light and shadow aspects of our true selves. In doing so, we empower ourselves to live consciously, powerfully, and courageously choose how we want to show up in the world."

JOCELYN WEISS, PHD, MPH, NBC-HWC

COURAGE TO
Shine

HOW TO FEEL
Confident
OUTSIDE YOUR
COMFORT ZONE

SARA REGESTER

Published by Deep Pacific Press
117 E 37th St. #580, Loveland, Colorado 80538

Deep
Pacific
Press

DeepPacificPress.com

email: sara@directions4wellness.com
www.Directions4Wellness.com

ISBN 978-1-956108-19-4 (paperback)
ISBN 978-1-956108-20-0 (eBook)

Cover design: Patrick Knowles
Interior design & formatting: Mark Thomas / Coverness.com

*This book is dedicated
in honor and celebration of
all my relations and Life's teachers.*

"For a seed to achieve its greatest expression, it must come completely undone. The shell cracks, its insides come out and everything changes. To someone who doesn't understand growth, it would look like complete destruction."

Cynthia Occelli

Contents

PROLOGUE

Stress is an inspiring subject. Being right there in the nitty gritty of your stress and resistance while coaching and conducting Stress Mastery workshops, I always see how stress and resistance dovetail together. I also get to witness the resilience of your feisty human spirit that, like the butterfly, is working to free your wings from your cocoon so you can take flight.

I was still practicing nursing when I had a life-changing epiphany about the undeniable connection between mind, body and spirit. It was 2 a.m. I stood at the bedside of my elderly patient as he lay awake, recovering from recent open-heart surgery. He said with a soft chuckle, "If I'd known I would live this long, I would have taken better care of myself."

He went on to tell a story of a lost love from his youth who had recently reached out to him in a letter, then proceeded to share how his life had not been what he had hoped it would be. I stood, my feet planted at his bedside, deeply listening to him reflect on his life. During those quiet, pensive moments, I witnessed him as he reconciled the life he had lived with the life he had hoped and dreamed.

Walking out of his room, I had the epiphany – this man with a physically broken heart had actually lived his life with an *emotionally* broken heart. I witnessed the mind-body-spirit showing how interconnected your emotional health is to your mind, your body and your spirit. His mind-body-spirit healing came when he was able to reconcile his lost dreams and aspirations from his past into the reality of the life he was living.

During the peaceful stillness of that night, my role of nurse shifted into that of a healer. With an open heart, I simply listened and held space for my elderly patient as he explored the truth residing within his Soul. In that moment, we shared a Soul-to-Soul connection as I witnessed the depth of his healing.

Stress is an invitation from Spirit to grow beyond our comfort zone so we can step into the unknown, from where it is possible to embody the greatest gifts of mind-body-spirit transformation.

As a healer, it is not my role to fix, but to hold a deeply intimate, open, heart-to-heart space for another. This is who I am as a heart healer. Heart medicine is my gift. In many ways, stress can be the symptom that manifests from broken heartedness, those large and small wounds encountered along life's journey that have not yet been integrated into lessons that provide an opportunity to gain wisdom and growth.

*

From the beginning, we are born into the mold of our family, culture, socioeconomics, religious or spiritual beliefs, and our nationality. The sex we are born into is another part of the mold that is chosen while still in spirit form, before we came into the physical of the persona we are living as now. From that mold, just as if we were a lump of malleable clay, we were sculpted by our parents, grandparents, siblings, teachers, and friends so we could fit in, conform, feel safe and survive.

We also experienced a variety of image makers (those who inspired us), and image takers (those who imprinted wounding that created pain patterns during our very early years).

At some level, while still in spirit, before we came into this lifetime through our mother's womb, we chose the mold we were born into to stack our deck for the most fertile opportunities to ensure personal growth and evolution during this lifetime.

> Ultimately, what we each learn in this lifetime is
> how we support the evolution of our immortal
> Soul towards enlightenment.

It is through our physical experiences in our body that our Soul evolves, and through our senses that we experience life in our physical body as a spiritual being.

Stress can be experienced, at the edge of our self-growth, any time we leave our comfort zone. Stress can wipe us out with the patterns we get stuck in, or alternatively, be seen as a direct opportunity from the Universe, God or who we identify with as our Higher Power for our personal growth and evolution.

> There is a demand for radical transformation in
> the collective consciousness as we experience
> the current polarizing climate in the world
> around us. The key to meeting this demand is to
> stop asking ourselves, "What am I going to do,"
> and instead ask, "How do I want to do this?"

This is how we step into self-responsibility to change our thoughts, habits and patterns. When we start living 180 degrees differently, we can create a new reality that is more "enlightened" as we increase our self-awareness and can assume authority for what is ours to do in the realm of change. We cannot change what happened in the past, but we can learn from the past, or shift our perspective about it, and choose how we want to live going forward.

Will you stand on the shore and wait for your ship to come in?

Will you stand by and blame the people and events around you for your current life situation?

Or will you step into the stream of livingness and start paddling for the distant shore with inner peace, knowing you are on track to heal your heart and claim your happiness?

STRESS AS OUR TEACHER

Health psychologist Kelly McGonigal, Ph.D., wrote *The Upside of Stress: Why Stress is Good for You, and How to Get Good at it,* which inspired my workshops and fertilized the birth of my Stress Mastery programs. Her book gave me the new science "make-over" for stress that correlated with what I understood metaphysically. In the chapters that follow, I transparently share with you what I have learned so you too may find a way to master your own stress.

A self-identified recovering stress junkie, I share my perspective as a registered nurse, integrative health coach, and international teacher of shamanism as an invitation to explore how you can transform your relationship with stress and see how it has been your teacher and guide throughout your life. My journey with stress, and what I learned in terms of my growth and healing at the edge of my stress, reveals what is behind the veil of stress in terms of the inner shadow that hides as a mask of stress. Here I share concepts of stress mastery versus stress wipe-out based on my own experience in Western medicine and have embedded teachings from my own path (an ancient shamanic lineage) into my story.

Stress often comes with change when we face the unknown, as well as our resistance in the face of change. There is positive stress (weddings, babies, anticipating a desired opportunity), negative stress (health issues, loss, overwhelm, unexpected change), and stress caused by poor design in the choreography of our lifestyle, such as when we overcommit ourselves or have the inability to say no. Stress can be harmful to us mentally, physically, and emotionally if we don't have a productive way to meet it.

> Stress is linked to what gives us meaning and
> purpose, as well as our personal values, because
> the things we care about most are often what
> trigger stress. But the new science of stress
> is clear – it's how we *think* about stress that
> determines if we harm or enhance our health
> and well-being.

It takes a holistic mind-body-spirit approach to train stress resilience as a mindset and lifestyle choice. As we wake up to become more aware of our circumstances and live more consciously, we can choose to take more responsibility for the choices by which we live. The more self-awareness we have, the greater the transformation that is possible. We can start taking responsibility for our happiness and harmony when we assume authority for how we want to live, even if it's making the smallest shifts in priorities or changes brought on through baby steps.

The good news – change is part of our natural human design.
Even the cells in our physical body are constantly changing to renew and recreate our physical self, while neuropathways are re-wiring and creating new connections in our nervous system as we make new patterns and habits.

We engage in change throughout our lifetime to evolve and grow at our own pace, from learning how to walk, talk, and ride a bicycle, to whatever we are integrating as our life lessons now. Any time we change our habits and patterns, we create a transformational experience that leads to our personal evolution.

We are essentially the "feet on the street" here in our present life, designed to evolve that part of us that has no body and is formless and immortal, known as our Spirit or Soul. Our Soul is very invested in supporting our continuous growth during this lifetime. It is the part of us that came into our physical body while in the womb as the spiritual being having a human-being experience.

We may ask ourselves *what is my purpose?* The simple answer is that we are here, living this lifetime, to evolve and grow as a person by whatever vehicle or platform we dreamed in for ourselves, be it a career, a passion, a partner, a parent or a friend. Stress will show up in any of these arenas of life experience where we are living by our values and what matters to us.

I wrote this book for you – the seeker, the lifelong learner, someone committed to your personal evolution and growth so you can achieve your highest potential. I have embedded spiritual concepts and knowledge that you can apply on your own path or use as a guide for your spiritual awakening.

We are in the evolutionary time of quickening, where many in the collective are waking up consciously and noticing the impact each of us has on our lives by taking responsibility for the choices we make.

> Complacency towards what we witness in the
> world can no longer be maintained as each of us
> reflects on the key question:
> "What is mine to do, and what really matters to
> me in my life?"

Recent times have been a wake-up call for most on our planet. This time of transformation is calling us to stretch beyond our personal focus into Soul consciousness, where we may be sensing more curiosity about our destiny and our role in serving a higher purpose as part of the solution.

With the earth going through changes in the environment, and world politics and economics coming under the spotlight, humanity is becoming more consciously awake as a collective and focused on truth and the desire to take a stand for what matters. This wave of change and awakening is unique to these times and has been building in intensity. We all feel the changes in the world around us, and for many it feels personal. This book brings the bigger picture back to us, and what we can do to not suffer the effects of stress induced by the many things beyond our control. We will explore what is behind the veil of our stress and what we can do to meet stress as a teacher and guide, so we may be more resilient in the face of our stress as we perceive it.

The invitation from our Soul, and the Universe, is for us to wake-up consciously to be more self-aware of both our shadow and our shining. There is so much to learn from self-exploration of both sides of our nature. Our shadow is that part of us that has adapted to life's challenges to cope, feel safe and survive. Our shadow patterns of thinking, emoting and behaving will sabotage our health, harmony and happiness, blocking our fullest expression of our shining and our gifts from the light. There is a point in the awakening of our consciousness where we gain self-awareness about these shadow patterns as dark reflections of our nature.

> The first step to healing our shadow is to shine
> the light into it, like shining a torch into a dark
> corner, then poke at it with curiosity to explore
> what is there for us to learn from.
> The challenge is to stay open to self-exploration
> so we can see the motivation behind it and
> understand the impact our dark side or shadow
> patterns have in our life.

These dark patterns of our shadow side are often hidden from our awareness in the form of strategies we adopted from wounding experienced during early childhood. Our shining side is our most authentic nature, that part of us that feels empowered and confident with inner security as we share our gifts. Our light side creates hope and connection to life, while our shadow side is our refuge, where we tend to disconnect from the present and open the door to hopelessness, depression, distraction, self-pity, and ultimately, a rejection of self. Which I came to recognize as broken heartedness that sabotages our happiness.

To heal, we must be willing to examine the conscious and unconscious limitations or shadow thoughts, feelings and patterns that block the expression of our natural gifts and shining. Healing our shadow will illuminate our talents, skills and abilities so we can share our authentic self brightly into the world to make an impact. Ultimately, exploring our shadow side allows us to integrate what happened in our past into wisdom we have learned from a place of self-acceptance, which brings self-compassion with deeper healing.

What we discover behind the veil of stress is both our light and our dark. The awakened self can choose to learn from pleasure and wisdom, rather than from pain, drama, and the self-pity of the victim.

**Life is a Vision Quest to explore and expand into
our potential.**

Our life teachers are all around us, in every arena of life. Our work is a spiritual practice if we are consciously awake and aware as we engage in our day. Our relationships at work and at home are the arenas where we gain some of our greatest life lessons, while our health will always get our attention with a demand to get back into balance and harmony.

Don't believe anything I say until you've tested the content from this book for yourself to see if these concepts work for you. I'm offering new perspectives, ideas, and tools for you to successfully meet your stress in a revolutionary way.

Freedom from stress comes when you step from
behind the veil of stress to fully express your
individuality. Behind the veil of stress, you may
find your shadow patterns of insecurity, fear
and resistance, or other sabotaging patterns of
thoughts and behaviors.

Autonomy, or to be self-governing, is not the same as self-reliance or independence. Autonomy is created through co-empowerment and having clear-cut boundaries and bottom lines within our agreements with self and others. I learned that stress really knocked me around because I had no agreements or bottom lines – I never spoke up for myself or took a stand against my tyrants. Rather than being true to myself, I gave my power to others and my work environments through co-dependency. I was profoundly impacted by the accumulation of stress in my life, simply because I soaked up stress like a sponge. I was a stress junkie from a very early age.

Stress mastery supports true individual, autonomous freedom, which can only happen through co-empowerment and a willingness to take a stand for our personal bottom lines.

And it starts here.

CHAPTER 1: YOU ARE A STRESS MAGNET

"The key is not to prioritize what's on your schedule, but to schedule your priorities."

Stephen Covey

In complete transparency, I'm a stress junkie, a stress magnet, and a self-proclaimed expert on how to be good at stress. Most people want to reduce their stress, and much has been written on managing stress, but my message is very different. I say, if we are living fully and completely engaged in those things that matter to us, we are going to have stress. Stress is linked to our meaning and those things we care about. Jon Kabat-Zinn, the father of mindfulness-based stress reduction (MBSR), described managing stress by saying, "You can't stop the waves, but you can learn to surf."

Stress is an inspiring topic once we truly understand the rules of engagement. As humans, we are naturally wired to change through access to the gift of free will to make different choices, yet we usually operate habitually from a well-worn path. My case states that most of us have hard-wired stress habits that have become our default stress loop. Mastering our stress so it works *for us,* not against us, is based on training new habits to rewire a stress-resilient response. The stress triggers may still show up, but how we respond to our stress is where the old stress habits can be transformed. My clients complete a validated assessment tool to measure their perceived stress at the start of our work together followed by a reassessment of their perceived stress at the completion of my Stress Mastery Program. Ultimately, my clients experience a markedly reduced perception of stress after they shift their stress response, even though the circumstances that induce stress may not have changed. This behavior outcome is what I refer to as Stress Mastery.

> I support my clients to *lean into* what is causing
> their stress with a new attitude and approach,
> to meet stress triggers with intention and
> empowerment, rather than falling victim to the
> effect of what is happening.

Stress mastery basics brings our awareness to the resistance that is often the cause of stress. Breaking the addiction to our stress habits starts when we are more aware of how we are responding to our stress triggers. Once we gain awareness, we can choose a new response to turn our stress around and become more resilient in the eye of the storm.

Let's look at some key points about the rules of engagement with stress:

- Our stress is triggered when something we care about is at stake. If we didn't care about it, we wouldn't be stressed.

- We feel triggered into stress by tyrants (those people and/ or events that push our buttons to create reactivity and energy loss).
- We can also feel stress when pressured by time, weather, traffic, or any number of challenges that come up in our day.
- There is also the stress invoked by change, such as implementing change at our job, moving to a new home, getting married or having a baby.

If we are living a fulfilling life, we will be faced with stress simply because our key values may compete with each other. For example, we want to go to the gym for exercise to support our value for health, but something comes up with work or family that is also an important priority. Stress may be triggered when we step into a new arena where we lack experience and confidence, creating feelings of vulnerability and fear from our insecurity. When we move through any new stage in life, such as moving away from home, embarking on a new career, parenting or entering retirement, we face unknown territory and feel stress. Each new phase has stress inherent in the chaos of the change as we navigate through our new life experiences.

> **It is not always possible to manage stress simply by getting rid of the cause. If those we care about are stressing us out, for example, our children, we are not likely going to get rid of them to reduce our stress; we simply need a more productive way to deal with them.**

On the other hand, when people say to me, "I'm good. I don't have any stress," I want to say back to them, "Your life must be boring, because you are not engaging with and learning from the things that give your life meaning and purpose." Typically, these individuals are likely cruising along in the safety of their comfort zone.

When we avoid stress, we are saying "no" to an opportunity to stretch and grow. We may say, "I would never do that because it would stress me out," which really means we are making a choice to stay in our comfort zone. Other times, we may distract, procrastinate, disconnect or sabotage with unhealthy behaviors to resist our stress. This may look like a Netflix® binge, scrolling social media, emotional eating, an extra beer, or glass of wine. We may busy ourselves in "safe tasks," those low-hanging fruit things we do, like cleaning our desk or doing housework to avoid engaging in what we are resisting that is stressful. In this case, we are just too busy catching up to deal with that big project right now.

Our values conflict with each other and compete for our time and attention, which is sure to open the door to stress if we are not clear about our priorities. For example, you're getting ready to leave work and head home when an important project from your boss or a client comes across your desk. You must make a decision, but it's more complex than it first appears. Do you stay late and support your value for your work priorities and support your team, or do you leave work on time to go to the park with your kids?

Let's say you make the decision to work late:

- First, you call your partner to see if they are willing to pick up the kids from daycare. (You're working late, so you won't get there on time.)
  First values conflict — my children are being raised by their daycare caregivers and not by me when I leave them there later than normal.
- The second values conflict happens when your partner says, "What! You're working late again???" Now you feel guilty about being a bad partner.

Time goes on and you finish the work project:

- Driving home, you realize you missed relaxing at the park with your kids which conflicts with your value for health and quality time with your family.
- You were going to cook a nice meal for your family and enjoy your time together, but now you need to pick up something quick to get dinner on the table, which goes against the value you have for nutritious home cooking.
- Like dominoes, your values, and the need to prioritize them, are bumped up against each other.

That's how easily stress can be triggered when so many things that matter to us in our day-to-day compete for our prioritization of focus, time, and what matters in terms of our values.

Many strategies will be offered throughout this book, but the short answer here is to take a deep breath, followed by a pause, and ask not, "What am I going to do?" but the more empowering question, "How am I going to do this?"

Our values will compete constantly, so it's important to discern which value is the priority today, because tomorrow it may be different. Today, the priority may be caring for this important work thing. Tomorrow, going home on time for your child's birthday dinner will be the priority. Is it getting to the yoga class because you've made a commitment to your health, or is it to stay late to help out a coworker on your team?

Our values are a moving target, so being flexible and spontaneous can support creative solutions to be able to say, "Yes, and…". This leaves us free to explore a compromise, or a creative solution, for both options, rather than always going to the polarizing place of choosing one value to the exclusion of the other. If I say *yes to this*, then I will have to say *no to that*.

> When we can mindfully tune into our values and
> what matters to us from a value perspective, we
> can prioritize with discernment to take decisive
> action without the guilt or "should," because
> we have more clarity of what is at stake as part
> of our values assessment. It's important to put
> all options on the table for a creative solution,
> rather than staying in a limiting view of tunnel
> vision.

Another way to recognize stress triggers is when we are feeling resistance to doing something. We can lose a lot of energy stressing about something we are resisting. An insightful question to ask when feeling stress is "What am I resisting?"

Any time we gain self-awareness, we can then gain clarity on how to address the problem. If we can discern what it is we are resisting about a particular stressful situation, we can then pick up a tool or a practice to get out of resistance. *Taking any step*, no matter how small, will lift the handbrake off our resistance. Seeing it clearly is the turning point, the moment we can choose to empower ourselves to take an action versus numbing out with a sabotaging behavior.

Personally, when I perceive stress about a project with a due date in the future, I will feel tension as tightness in my gut and naval. I feel the stress *physically in my body* before I'm aware of my mind thinking about it. As I tune in, I'm able to name what it is I'm resisting. If there's a work project I need to prepare for, I can procrastinate and find some distracting "busy" work to do, such as reading emails or articles, getting a snack, or calling a friend. By engaging in these activities, I can start to feel mental anxiety and worry about the neglected work project. None of these choices are a good use of my time or energy resources, but with a couple of centering breaths in my lower belly (below my naval), I can reboot myself into the present moment. Now I can have the discernment with clarity of what one step I can take in order to take action and step out of my resistance.

Once I get started on the project, my resistance is reduced and I perceive less stress. The project is still there, the timeline still has a hard stop, but I'm moving forward into flow and taking off the brakes that could stop my forward movement.

**Flow starts when I take responsibility for my
first step.**

Additionally, there are more productive ways to meet stress triggers than always going to the default of the fight-or-flight mode of stress response where we rev our system into high gear with our hormone response. Culturally, we have encoded the belief that stress is bad and too much will harm us physically or wipe us out energetically. Many people habitually react to stress with the default of fight-or-flight stress response, which triggers their survival instinct every time they feel stress, even when there is no true life-threatening danger. Biologically this is like using a sledgehammer to kill a fly when a fly swatter would have done the job.

If we just had a blow up with a family member in the kitchen, or if we're having a bad day at work, we don't need to go to the fight-or-flight stress response. Doing so releases a surge of stress hormones that will continue to flog the organs and bathe the cells for as long as the threat is perceived (survival mode). Chemically and hormonally, the sympathetic nervous system prepares us physically to either fight for our life or run for our life. When we chronically respond to stress triggers this way, the effect on the body will result in health problems over time.

When we have alternative ways to respond to stress triggers, we can reduce the release of the stress-inducing hormones and firing of the sympathetic nervous system. Triggering the parasympathetic nervous system (called the rest-and-digest response) will slow down the heart rate and support all the organ systems to function more effectively, like putting on the brakes. Practicing a new approach and adopting a new attitude to shift our mindset to support stress-resilient responses to our stress triggers, means although the triggers may still come, our perception shifts our stress response.

To describe how our system shifts into survival adaptability when we are under a perceived or real threat is to understand there is intricate communication that happens between the sympathetic nervous system and the adrenal-cortical system that carries hormones and neurotransmitters through the blood stream to target various tissues and organs. The checks and balances of this internal response are very sensitive, like a hair trigger on a pistol. The overall effect is that the body becomes tense and revs up, like stepping on the gas pedal, and we become more mentally alert to focus on the threat in front of us. System-wide there are many shifts and changes to prepare for fighting or fleeing for your life.

You can imagine how stress gets a bad rap when we get caught up in the collective mindset about stress. Many of us have been habitually over-relying on the fight-or-flight stress response as the default mode for every daily situation that we have internally encoded as a threat to our safety. The mindset and practices for stress resilience are the new responses to train, like exercising to develop muscle memory. Science has shown that how we think about stress has a huge impact on our health and happiness.

As described in *The Upside of Stress: Why Stress is Good for You and How to Get Good at It* by Kelly McGonigal, Ph.D., there are three stress responses. Each has a unique way to support us when we are triggered by stress, and if we use these responses, we can learn and grow from our stress. Using these alternative modes of stress response will take practice and awareness to retrain a new habitual way to respond to stress (I have emphasized these alternative stress responses throughout this book, with permission from the author). You can read about the latest science of stress and resilience studies in *The Upside of Stress.*

1. Meet-the-Challenge Response

This is the response we want to train up as our new way (except for those moments there is truly a danger or threat). We don't have to run out of burning buildings on a daily basis, but daily triggers from the people or events at work and at home may open the door to our stress.

The meet-the-challenge response gives us the boost of energy needed to focus and feel motivated for action, but the stress-related hormones don't stay elevated in a way that leads to inflammation and harm to our body. This response will help us rise to the occasion and meet the challenge successfully, with full access to our mental and physical resources.

> Meet-the-challenge response supports learning
> from the engagement.

We may identify with feeling anxious, but actually we are excited because we want to do well as we meet the challenge. Using the meet-the-challenge response, we can integrate the experience to learn from it. An example of meet-the-challenge response is when an athlete has butterflies in their stomach, sweaty palms and a rapid heart rate, but they are looking forward to the big game and want to perform well. Another example is for anyone who has studied for an important exam. Using the meet-the-challenge response they can test well and learn from what they have studied.

In contrast, a person who identifies as a poor test taker is likely going into the fight-or-flight stress response mode. They go into tunnel vision, encode that taking a test is a threat, and with all the symptoms of anxiety, may freeze during their test and not recall what they studied. The key strategy here is any time we feel a threat or anxiety about a stressful situation, we can turn it around and feel more courage when we reframe our perspective using the meet-the-challenge response to transform fear into courage, which creates a stress-resilient physiology of the hormone response in the body, specifically impacting the cortisol and adrenaline levels.

An example of how we can implement the meet-the-challenge attitude as a response is when we are feeling anxious or nervous about an upcoming event. We can pause and ask ourselves, "Am I excited, or am I anxious?" Then we can talk ourselves off the ledge of the anxiety cliff and shift our attitude out of anxiety. "I am excited because this is an amazing opportunity and I hope I do really well. I can only get better from here."

Encoding feelings of excitement will lift our mood and support access to the meet-the-challenge mode of stress resilience. It turns the inner critic into "Yes! I can do this." It's very empowering to reframe anxiety into excitement. The body will shift the anxious energy when you label your frame of reference differently.

2. Tend-and-Befriend Stress Response

The tend-and-befriend stress response biologically motivates the social caregiving system and increases social relationships and connection, helping us to bond and support one another. Regulated by the bonding hormone oxytocin (one of our primary stress resilience factors), when this system is activated, we feel more empathy, connection and trust. This hormone will also decrease fear and increase courage. Think about what a parent will do to save their child from harm, accessing supernatural strength and putting aside any concern for their own risk. This stress response not only reduces fear, but increases hope, which will naturally increase resilience.

The more we connect with others to offer or
receive support, the more this response can
help us to feel confidence and courage to meet
adversity. The tend-and-befriend response
releases a cascade of hormones that make us
social, brave, and smart so we can take action.

We access tend-and-befriend every time we lean in for support, offer support to another, or find meaning from something we are dealing with. We access this mode when we come together to grieve at a funeral, when we tell stories, share food and support one another in our grief. We access this when we lean into our peers or supporters at work to share our challenges or losses, or when we come together in community during a crisis, sharing with our partner about our challenges, or meeting a friend for a coffee. This response is what motivates a sense of community and coming together. We can also access courage and confidence through our spiritual practice when we lean into something greater than ourselves. In Dr. McGonigal's words, "the tend-and-befriend response makes us brave and social."

3. Fight-or-Flight Stress Response

This stress response is intended to trigger our survival instinct to fight for our life or run away. If we wake up and our house is engulfed in flames, or if we're driving our car and swerve to avoid a car accident, this stress response will kick in immediately to ensure our survival. Notice when a real threat happens how you feel in the moment when the shock hits, and how quickly it dissipates after the threat has resolved. Initially, we feel the generalized shake of fine tremors, followed by the wave of relief as the energy dissipates.

In this response to danger, the neurotransmitter and hormone surge will give us tunnel vision to focus on the threat. Our blood is shunted to the vital organs that need increased blood supply to take action, and our heart rate and blood pressure increase to pump the blood faster under higher pressure to deliver life-saving oxygen to the vital organs, brain and muscles. Our body releases stored blood sugar for extra fuel, while other systems such as digestion, reproduction and immune system function are shut down to conserve energy during survival mode. The body is supercharged, with stress hormones bathing the cells and flogging the organs for the duration needed to face the threatening situation.

During this response, the only thing we are learning is to identify the threat to our physical safety. This mode is not conducive to learning from the experience. This is what happens when individuals freeze during an exam – they are in survival mode, not learning mode. The more effective stress response is to access the meet-the-challenge response or the tend-and-befriend response, rather than always relying on the fight-or-flight response, which is physically exhausting and emotionally draining.

One final point from Dr. McGonigal's book worth noting refers to the current research on stress. Studies have shown that it's not the stress triggers themselves that create poor outcomes from stress, but *how we think* about stress that will determine our health and happiness (Keller, et. al. 2012). The studies identified that individuals who live a "stressful" life and perceive that stress is harmful, will have more health problems during aging and live a shorter life. These individuals may be thinking, "This stress is going to kill me," which puts them into the fight-or-flight stress response. The other profile relates to individuals who live equally demanding lives but do not believe that stress is harmful. These individuals have an attitude of "Wow, I'm really busy, how will I get through this?" These people by nature have a more resilient attitude, use the meet-the-challenge response, and live longer with fewer health problems.

It takes consistent practice to encode a new habit and to break the old program. Neuroplasticity, the re-wiring process used to create new habits and patterns, takes 66-90 days. Repetition and consistency over time will create new neuropathways so you can integrate a new way to meet life when triggered by stress.

The following metaphor demonstrates how we re-wire our brain to create new neuropathways that support new patterns and habits. Imagine we are walking along a trail in nature. It's a well-defined trail, effortless to travel as we walk, chatting with our hiking companion. Suddenly, we see interesting landscape off to the left. You say, "Let's go that new way." So, we leave the defined trail and forge a new path off to the left. We must be mindful and aware where we are stepping as we find our way, paying attention with every step over the barriers and obstacles on our path.

The next time we go hiking, we choose to follow that same way to the left. Each time we take that new path, the trail gets more clearly defined and takes less effort to follow. We can relax more and remember the new path we are following as a second attention while we're chatting on the trail. No longer used, the old path will fade away and become absorbed back into the forest as a faint track. The joy and pleasure we feel on the new path motivates us to stay on the new course until it becomes the new default way, or habit, as a well-traveled trail.

This is how our brain works to make a new pathway when we develop a new pattern of behavior or habit. We are designed to re-wire neuropathways through neuroplasticity, or flexibility of the brain that creates new connections of nerve cells that support new growth and change.

When we commit to the new way and abandon the old pathway, we will build a new channel for communication between nerve cells that informs how we will adopt a new thought or behavior. We develop a new habit or behavior when we consistently practice the new way. We can create more connecting links if we associate pleasure and fun to our learning process, which feels motivating, like something we *want* to do, rather than feeling resistance to something we *should* do.

If we want to stop the habit of being reactive every time we are triggered by stress, we must commit to creating the new path for responding to stress without the habitual emotional discharge and energy loss.

At the core of stress resilience are two key factors which will be expanded on in later chapters:

1. Training presence so we can be in the present moment, centered in our body, with balanced, neutral or non-judgmental emotions. This refers to a method or practice to drop into our center physically, and out of our head mentally, so we can bypass the inner critic and be anchored in the space with focus.

2. Training mindfulness, also called mindful awareness, to be able to pause, reflect and give ourselves enough internal space to tune into our awareness. Then we may ask ourselves, "How will I deal with this?" or, "What are my options?" so we can bypass the habitual reactive stress response of emotional discharge and energy loss.

There are a number of ways to train presence and mindful awareness. It's for each of us to find what works for us individually. They are commonly referred to as practices for a reason – they need to be practiced so we can encode them into a new pattern or habit.

Picking up tools and practices to train an
attitude of resilience is how we create a lifestyle
that supports our happiness, health, humor,
hope and harmony.

CHAPTER 2: HEAL YOUR BROKEN HEART

"Physician, heal thyself."

Luke 4:23

We often feel stress when we feel conflict about pleasing others with "should-dos" versus following our heart's desire with "want-to-dos." What I learned about myself as I recapitulated the stories and memories from my past highlights that when I was very young, there were many peak emotional experiences where I attempted to speak up for myself or to state my feelings or opinions, and they were not heard or valued. In fact, my voice was often overruled by my friends, parents, siblings, teachers, my friends' parents, etc. A repeating theme of my childhood, it created wounding that I brought forward into adulthood. I was given a clear message that it was not safe to speak up for myself, to ask for what I wanted, or to take a stand to clarify my point of view. I recognize that the impact of my emotional trauma was that I was brokenhearted. I didn't love myself, and I didn't accept myself, so I looked outside myself for approval and acceptance.

Some of these memories are highlighted in this book to illustrate how I developed patterns of over-giving, over-working and co-dependency from a place of wanting to feel safe, accepted and loved. Ultimately, being unable to speak up for myself, I lacked self-respect and became complacent to the will of others by giving my power away.

I was constantly doing things from a desire to "fix" myself. My journey to master my stress is how I healed my broken heart. The irony is that I was a cardiac nurse for many years, helping my patients with physically broken hearts. Part of my spiritual awakening to my destiny is based on what I witnessed in my patients and clients, who I recognized also had broken hearts energetically related to a mind-body-spirit nature.

These were compelling motivators to pick up the unskilled behavior patterns and beliefs about myself that reflected that I was just not good enough. So, I set forth to prove my value and my worth to myself, life and others by pushing myself for excellence and perfection in everything I did. My insecurity was the door that laid the foundation for becoming a stress junkie and stress magnet. These patterns would eventually take out my health and sabotage my key relationships. Over many years, I have learned to master my stress and heal my heart.

We can feel so much stress and resistance when we don't speak up, holding onto our thoughts, ruminating and imagining what we would say. The skill of honest, heart-to-heart communication can turn around relationships of any sort, and starts with skills for mindful listening. Repression energy blocked my communication and my actions from being heartfelt and true, as I always tried to say and do what I thought the other person wanted me to because I needed to maintain emotional safety.

As a stress junkie, I had multiple stress-induced health experiences working as a nurse. Many times, I wiped out my health and burned myself out. I always said yes. I had no boundaries or bottom lines to say no and didn't know how to say no without feeling waves of guilt and insecurity. Consequently, I always covered shifts when we were short-staffed because I felt responsible and believed they needed me and no one else could do it. I took care of the sickest or most complex patients because I was reliable. l was asked to lead special projects as I was the one with follow-through who could track the details. Dependable, success-driven, and willing to take on extra responsibilities, I ran circles around my colleagues and was acknowledged for my high energy. My peers teased me for being such a maniac at work. My bosses loved me because I was so productive.

I had a successful career, but my work environment was toxic, and more significantly, the way I was working was harming my health. I would focus on my healing to feel better, then go back into my stress patterns of pushing and striving for success, which attracted new health problems. My immune system took the hit in numerous ways with autoimmune dysfunction.

I was a co-dependent, over-giving, rescuing, enabling workaholic on the inside and a success-driven, highly motivated and respected healthcare professional on the outside. No one could see how unhealthy I was because of the way I lived life fully and showed up with a very strong, productive, and capable outer shell. I was addicted to the approval and acknowledgment I received from others and completely disconnected from my inner heart's desires.

The pushing and striving to prove my self-worth and to take on challenges had a price. I didn't develop the alcohol addiction that ran in my family, but my over-giving and over-working depleted both my physical health and my mental-emotional well-being. My life and my body were out of balance and this combination had a profound impact on my health. During the phase of my career as a nurse from 1986-2000, I had multiple systems with symptoms. Oddly, I didn't feel exhausted but rather I was hyperactive on overdrive, yet unfocused. Pale, thin, and malnourished, I had global issues with symptoms of food allergies, environmental allergies, latex allergy, nervous system issues with fine motor compromise, depression, anxiety, foggy brain and memory issues, dental issues, weight loss, dysmenorrhea, and focus/attention deficit issues. I had severe immune system challenges that triggered asthma, herpes, and leaky gut syndrome, and eventually, my thyroid and adrenals took the hit, too.

I was a mess. I didn't even recognize my symptoms until someone else pointed them out and referred me to an Environmental Medicine Physician Specialist. I remember my referring physician said, "It may be too late for you." *That sobering moment made me recognize how sick I was, yet because of my deeply rooted pattern of self-reliance and pushing myself to please others from my lack of self-respect and self-care, I'd been able to go to work and function like everything was fine.* But nothing about my life was ok. I underwent many months of diagnosis and treatment to detox my body and boost my immune system.

> I learned the process of healing from my own
> healing journey. Healing comes in layers
> through a multi-pronged, holistic approach
> beyond just treating the physical symptoms.

My strongest healing came from the ways I changed my beliefs, and opened and shifted my mindset to change my patterns of behavior.

The more I evolved personally, the healthier I became. I evolved in my personal growth from each personal journey with my health, like a spiral lifting me up to my next level. My healing was a process that evolved over time; it was not an overnight miracle.

I was a changed person once I got to the other side of that healing journey. Following the rigorous program my doctor gave me, I experienced a much-improved state of health. Over time, as I continued to do my inner work, all the symptoms completely resolved. Once I started on the spiritual path of my shamanic studies in 2003, I continued the healing process in mind-body-spirit, layer by layer. Even today my healing journey continues to evolve even deeper. I needed the Western medicine physician who specialized in training to diagnose and address my issues. I needed the diagnostic tools, the prescribed interventions, medications and, in this case, the supplements and dietary changes. But what really kicked up the mental and emotional healing process were all the other things I did to heal my heart. I began to feel more self-acceptance and gain a stronger connection to empowerment through my spiritual practices, including healing through ceremonial experiences, where I was able to drop deeply into my inner wisdom to heal those extremely hidden parts of myself.

As I healed from those major health problems, I had two epiphanies or "ah-ha" moments. First, in learning to heal myself from life's stress and my health problems, I realized I could help others to heal themselves. Second, I used a multi-pronged mind-body-spirit approach, and discovered I didn't have to treat my symptoms with Western medicine alone. Western medicine became a bridge to all the other pieces that contributed to my greater healing.

At the heart of my healing journey was my
willingness to take responsibility for my
healing and to learn about myself through self-
discovery from the afflictions in my body that
were my teachers.

The afflictions taught me to be more receptive, more spontaneous, and more present and anchored in my womb within my body, not just living in my intellect above my chin. They taught me to speak up and to listen to my heart's desire. I was a coachable and willing student. It was my connection to my spiritual practice, prayer, intention, and connection to nature that supported my journey. My health problems came as a knock from Spirit. At first the knock was soft, but as I tuned it out and ignored my physical vulnerabilities, the knock became louder until I was stopped in my tracks with a major health crisis.

Here's the nugget – the body is in the mind. Like the expression "Physician, heal thyself," we all have the capacity to heal when we take responsibility for our own healing journey. Our physical body is controlled by our consciousness in terms of how we think, what we think, and the intention for healing that we focus on. "The body is in the mind" means that it is possible to determine our own healing if we are willing to take on new growth in some way. The ability to heal is within all of us.

The key to our healing comes from within, not from a healer on the outside. We are our own healer; the doctor or practitioner is really our guide or supporter. Healing doesn't come when we put blame on something or someone. Healing evolves when we take responsibility for our choices and focus on what we can always change – our attitude about how we think about life and the approach or action we take to engage with it.

Attention = Power

Where we place our attention is what grows. Are we placing our attention on being sick, or are we focused on our healing? This is what my journey taught me, and what I teach you.

Some people are given a diagnosis and just accept the identity or label as who they are with that health problem, never questioning or considering there may be something about it they can change.

> If we never question what we can learn from our health problem, or explore what it is teaching us, we may not evolve back into health and balance.

By balance, I'm referring to balancing the five aspects of being human. We are emotional, physical, mental, spiritual, and sexual beings. If we are out of balance in any of these aspects, we may open the door to health problems. Healing itself may or may not be physical. There may be healing of the other four aspects mentioned above. Healing comes when we are willing to engage in change holistically; therefore, we can heal ourselves when we put attention on what we can change in terms of how our inner attitude and approach can re-wire behaviors or patterns to come back into balance. Balance is experienced when we can measure improved happiness, health, humor, hope and harmony.

However, in my experience for myself and my clients, healing is not a one-way path. Healing comes when we know what we are dealing with in terms of a diagnosis and are able to take in whatever treatments or modalities support the symptoms. All the other things we do on our healing journey to change our pattern, to shift our mindset and to change our lifestyle in new ways are all part of the journey to heal. It's not one thing that brings healing, but everything we do to engage the mind, body and spirit to heal. We evolved into a health problem over time, which is why it takes time to transform our patterns and live life in a new way to evolve out of a health problem. This is, energetically, like a spiral movement.

Healing may be on a physical, mental, emotional, and spiritual level and will impact our life force energy, also known as chi or ki. Healing is many layers deep, and ultimately, when we engage in life with a health problem it will be our teacher who will guide us to learn and grow. We may still have physical symptoms that may be less frequent or less severe, and we may notice other parts of our life are transformed through our attention and care for our physical. I witnessed this process in my patients diagnosed with heart disease. When a person with a cardiovascular diagnosis starts changing their diet, exercising more, losing weight, stops smoking and gets their stress mastered, that individual is living their life in a whole new pattern. They will have a new outlook, a new attitude and a new approach to life. That person may still have heart disease to some degree, but they are now living life in a more balanced, fulfilling way, a way to live happier.

We can't assume what form the healing will take, but we can stay open and receptive to the process of change. The key for healing is how we actively take responsibility for our actions towards change.

Healing doesn't happen *to us*. It happens with
our clear intent and follow-through when
taking steps towards change. We must be an
active participant in the process.

Let me share about a client with a chronic nervous system disease. Every time she pushed herself with stress in her business her physical symptoms flared up, forcing her to walk with a cane, sit in a wheelchair or become bedridden with exhaustion. Once she learned how to master her stress, she started seeing her life change. Her marriage became more fulfilling as she approached her relationship in a new way, with renewed energy. Her business was able to grow, and her diminished symptoms didn't stop her in her tracks. Her healing came when she managed her energy levels, ate healthier with better planning, and most significantly, when she added more fun, spontaneity and creativity into her life to balance her analytical left-brain job demands. Her healing was based on balancing her day with the things she loved to do that didn't happen when she was stressed and overworking. Today, her business is thriving, her marriage is strong, and she is able to manage her growing business without wiping herself out.

Healing came when she let her busy mind pause
to listen to her body and followed through on
the many small changes she made from her
inner guidance. Her disease has taught her how
to listen to what her body needs to stay healthy,
whole, balanced and creative.

I did many things to promote my self-healing. I was open to new ideas and tried new ways of doing things, including going to new practitioners for acupuncture, massage, energy work, and chiropractic. I saw a medical intuitive in my early days who gave me deep insight, along with practices I could do to stay focused on my healing. I spent time in nature, and I had a shamanic healing ceremony designed to get at both the symptoms and the cause of my afflictions. I took workshops, read books to learn new ways, and I changed my diet whilst adding supplements to boost my immune system.

My self-care translated into all the ways that I started taking responsibility for my health and happiness by making changes that impacted my mind-body-spirit. As I shifted to a new mindset and prioritized to create new lifestyle patterns, my symptoms got milder and less frequent.

> The stronger my connection was to my spiritual
> growth, the healthier, happier and more
> balanced I became.

Layer by layer, I peeled away at the onion, healing holistically and re-wiring my stress junkie patterns into co-empowerment, with bottom lines and boundaries, as well as a balance of the feminine and masculine energies within myself to be more receptive. I continue on this journey to heal new depths within myself.

When we heal our life, our health gets better. Health is not a linear process, but an interconnection with our emotional, mental, spiritual and creative expression of our Soul force or creative spark in our life.

Practice: Guided Imagery to Focus on Healing

During my healing journey, I used guided imagery to connect with my physical body and focus my attention and intent on my healing. You can do this in a meditative way, or by simply spending a few minutes picturing your afflicted physical area within your imagination.

Here is an example of how I used guided imagery when I was diagnosed with Graves' disease and developed nodules on my thyroid gland that created hyperthyroidism:

- Taking a deep breath, I would drop my attention into my center, between my second and third chakra, located 2-3 finger breadths below my naval and a bit back towards my spine. (Our second chakra is key to our will and will power.)
- I would close my eyes and imagine my thyroid gland.
- I then talked to my thyroid, asking it to heal the nodules for a smooth surface.
- I pictured my thyroid gland surface as pink, healthy and smooth.
- I would then ask my thyroid to secrete the exact level of thyroid hormones that I needed to maintain a healthy metabolism. Not too much, not too little, but the exact amount I needed.

For me, the bridge to heal my overactive thyroid was oral medication. The endocrinologist wanted to irradiate my thyroid gland initially, but I asked if there were other options and started on the medication and regular check-ups. Over time, the oral medication was weaned off and my thyroid nodules healed. I had a repeat scan ten years later and my thyroid is still stable, without any evidence of hyperactivity.

The guided imagery was a powerful approach, using my imagination to see, know, and trust that I was healing. By conversing with my thyroid gland, it became my teacher to teach me what I needed to learn to heal my concepts of self, feel more self-acceptance, and have more self-awareness so I could focus on my healing. I have used the guided imagery to connect and communicate with my physical body to heal from other afflictions, too.

> Attention = Power. This practice puts out a clear
> intent to heal and to be receptive to what our
> teacher, the physical body, is teaching us as we
> restore our balance and harmony.

CHAPTER 3: FROM CATHOLICISM TO SHAMANISM

"Watch your thoughts, for they will become
actions. Watch your actions, for they'll
become... habits. Watch your habits for
they will forge your character. Watch your
character, for it will make your destiny."

Margaret Thatcher

I was raised Catholic, part of a long lineage of Irish Catholics who migrated to America during the potato famine to find a better life. Attending Catholic school for thirteen years before I went to university to study nursing, I felt such a strong connection to Spirit through prayer from an early age that I often mused about becoming a nun. I was intrigued by the mysticism of Catholic rituals and traditions, from the scent of incense burning, the sound of chimes ringing or chanting during high mass, and the elaborate artistry of the accoutrement on the altar. I read about the lives of saints just for fun, inspired by their acts of courage and manifestation of miracles. My mother was my first spiritual teacher and taught me how to pray, how to ask for what I want through prayer and to believe in angels, saints and the mystery of the Holy Spirit.

When I was young, there were limited but common career options for young women. Many of us grew up to be nurses and teachers. The nuns of my high school would joke that they were saving a room for me in the convent. I think my mother went along with it, but secretly hoped I would get married and produce grandchildren, neither of which came to pass.

I was a happy, fulfilled Catholic. I went to mass every Sunday, observed the sacraments and was spiritually guided by the Jesuits and the BVM order of Sisters who were my teachers. My family was always very well connected with the Catholic Church in the ways they supported the Parish and the schools. Father Thom, a dear friend of my family, was like an uncle to me and celebrated the weddings and baptisms in our circle of family and friends. He had a gift to make those celebrations very heartfelt and personal. He was dearly loved by all and was known to be the gregarious life of the party.

My grandparents founded a retail furniture business in our town in the 1940s. Before I was born, my grandfather donated nightstands to the hospital convent for the sisters who ran the hospital. He also completely decorated and furnished a waiting room as a designated place for family to wait while the mothers were in labor. After I was born, my parents never received a bill for my delivery. When they inquired at the hospital, Sister Placita said, "Don't worry about your bill. Sara is on us!" Years later, I worked at that same Catholic hospital for most of my nursing career.

My family, along with another family, lived on a ranch in the

Colorado Rockies every summer from June through August. Every Sunday morning, all nine of us piled into the station wagon and drove to town, staving off carsickness from the winding dirt road to go to church. Other times, when my mother invited her favorite priests to visit, we held mass on the ranch. Father Thom and other Jesuits from our school in Phoenix would come and offer mass at home. My mother is the only person I know who stored communion wafers in the freezer and stashed a special box of altar accoutrement on the closet shelf to have on hand for the occasions when a visiting priest celebrated Mass with us on the ranch.

Growing up within my Catholic culture was a positive experience. I never imagined I would drift in another direction. It was nearly a surprise when, in 2002, shamanism found me. I didn't go looking for a new path or a new way. My experience happened in an organic, evolutionary way that shifted how I now practice my faith and connection to Spirit. Part of me still honors the Catholic tradition, as it is the foundation of my spiritual roots.

Although I describe my Catholic upbringing as positive, that's not to say there weren't hard lessons along the way, or that I didn't have to escape from the cultural or heritage mold that included alcohol addiction, guilt, blame, shame, and issues around sexual repression. That was all part of the package and the programming in which I grew up. I am not a person who experienced an epiphany moment of spiritual awakening, or a dark night of the Soul crisis, as I don't remember a time when I didn't feel connected to Spirit and part of creation. My family prayed together at dinner, and from the time I was a tiny girl, my mother sat on my bed every night before I went to sleep as I knelt and said my bedtime prayers.

Mind-Body-Spirit Connection

Throughout my work at the hospital, the mind-body-spirit connection of the patients I cared for always fascinated me. I was intrigued by the backstory my patients shared as they reflected on their current health crisis in terms of the scope and current circumstances of their life. Reading patient histories, I was curious about the connection of their life in terms of the synchronicity of events that brought them to the hospital.

For example, I cared for a police officer who came to the cardiac unit with a rapid, irregular heartbeat, three days following his retirement. He and his wife shared with me that they had recently purchased an RV and were looking forward to touring around America. On his second day in the unit, he unexpectedly coded and died before he could enjoy the dream of his new chapter. I reflected on the irony of the timing and circumstances of his life and unexpected death.

Patients like these made me curious about the human condition when faced with life-threatening illnesses. Why would one person succumb, despite the best care, and another could meet every confrontation and heal back into life? Over time, I learned that we are spiritual beings having a human-being experience. I caught glimpses of the human spirit that showed up at times of deep crisis. How connected we are to that part of our spiritual self is very individual. I saw the spirit inside my patients during those intimate moments, when they were open and vulnerable, and most obviously during the life and death transitions I witnessed.

My curiosity about the timing of one's life and death, and the mystery of the Soul's journey after one's physical life ended, opened me up to the idea that life goes on after we leave our physical body. I could imagine that we get to come back into another lifetime to do it a little better next time, and how reincarnation made sense in terms of the evolution of the immortal Soul. This was not what I learned in theology class!

Death is a mystery. Culturally, few people want to talk about death, or face it. I'm the one who has always been curious about it. I was moved by the courage I observed through the life and death process and the resiliency of the human spirit I witnessed throughout my nursing career, and by the doctors, nurses and chaplains who supported the patients and their families.

Shamanism has a different perspective about death. It teaches that death will always bring new life through rebirth and renewal. In shamanism, energy never dies or goes away, it transforms. Death is not only associated with physical death, but is also part of the little deaths of change that are part of the death-change-transformation process in daily living. In nature you can see the death-change cycles every autumn when the leaves change color and fall off the trees. Trees are dormant throughout winter, appearing dead, then in spring they bud with new leaves, as new life. The summer trees are in full foliage before the leaves turn again and fall off in autumn. These cycles of death-change-transformation are always moving as part of nature. And so it is with the human experience.

The paradox of death is that it is not all about the ending, because it is also transforming into a new beginning.

The old form or pattern may die so the new form can be created. In shamanism, we say we want to make death an ally. This means we want to invite the death-change-transformation process to allow what is no longer serving us to die so we can open to something new.

Any form of healing is an example of death-change-transformation.

In the context of healing, someone diagnosed with a serious health issue who chooses to modify their lifestyle to focus on their healing will go through a death process to let their old ways die so they can create new, healthier lifestyle patterns. This person evolves to live with a new attitude and approach toward their life as they recover and heal by allowing their old ways to transform into their new lifestyle through rebirth and renewal. Through this entire change process, they are rewriting their story from a new perspective and training their free will muscle to make new choices. As we say in the shamanic healing paradigm, change your life and your health gets better.

Death will always awaken our desire for new life through rebirth and renewal. Life and death are like two sides of a coin. Through death, new life is born in the form of change or transformation. When we eat food, even vegetables, that food dies so that we may live. When we allow something to end in our life, new doors will open and new opportunities will present. When we decide to change a pattern or habit, a new or better way may be possible. As humans, we are constantly meeting some form of death, change, and transformation. This is part of how we evolve and grow throughout our lifetime.

We see it in nature, we see it in our everyday life, and we witness it when we experience the physical death of others in our life, their passing impacting us with change. The person who "crosses over" will return to spirit and depart this physical world, but their Spirit, or the essence of who they are, will continue in formlessness and freedom from their physical body. That person is essentially rebirthing themselves from a substance or physical form into the formlessness of Spirit. It's the natural cycle of life. As a nurse I witnessed this, and it was through shamanism that I came to understand death as part of a natural cycle of life. They are not separate from each other, but two sides of a coin. Life and death is a paradox.

The connection to healing and the mind-body-spirit was something I witnessed in my patients and experienced for myself. It was through the study of shamanism that I understood how we are naturally designed to evolve and grow, and that sometimes our greatest personal growth comes from how we seek our personal healing beyond our physical aspect, to include our emotional, mental, spiritual and sexual aspects of self. These are referred to as the five aspects of being human.

Allow me to elaborate on the qualities of our sexual energy as a catalyst. Our sexual aspect is linked to our life force energy, the essence of our individuality and creativity, and is measured as our chi or ki. It's through our sexual Soul force energy that we catalyze change and transformation. It is the spark of our individuality that *is the essence of everything we create and has our stamp of creativity beyond physical babies.*

We are much more than the mind-body that is often referred to in holistic medicine. Studying shamanism gave me the wisdom to understand how to connect to nature to heal through the elements, the mineral world, the plant world, the animal world, and all of creation as a resource circle to access for healing, layer after layer, through many years of my studies and ceremonial experiences.

*

The door to shamanism opened to me very innocently when I was forty-two years old. On a rainy night on the other side of town, I arrived late to a women's networking event. One of the women there passed some smudge around the women's circle. It was a smoky herbal mixture of sage, cedar, and lavender. This was a new experience for me, so I joined in the ritual when the smoking abalone shell and feather fan were passed to me. We all shared, one-by-one, an experience from our past. The group sharing was followed by testimonials from women who had attended a spiritual workshop. I went home that night with the workshop brochure literally clutched to my chest and submitted my registration the next day.

In January 2003, I attended the workshop and had my first exposure to shamanism. My experience was both profound and sobering. I saw clearly that I felt chronically ill and depressed, which awakened the hunger in me to dive deep into my Soul and heal those darkest parts that kept me stuck in my stress patterns: working all the time, not dating, and being underweight with a severely impacted immune system. I recognized how out of touch I was with my feminine receptive side, as I was living in the pattern of being an overactive doer.

I heard this prayer spoken by the teachers which, following the workshop, echoed in my core and awakened my curiosity:

"Everything is born of woman and sparked by
man, and nothing must be done to harm the
children. In honor and celebration of life and
the people..."

I experienced three more ceremonial workshops over the next few months, each revealing a profound depth of insight into how I kept trying to be perfect, and the patterns of taking on difficult or almost impossible challenges as a way to feel my value and competence. For me, something that was easy didn't even seem worth doing. Proving my self-worth by pushing through challenges and striving for perfection was the pattern that was wiping out my health. I was living in the negative – or what I refer to as the shadow side of challenge. I see this pattern in my clients too. You may also relate to the impact on you as a person who tries to keep up this unrealistic life of doing hard things to feel good enough, or worthy of self-acceptance, through outside approval from others.

In contrast to all my pushing and striving, the ceremonial workshops helped me imagine who I really wanted to be – empowered, confident, passionate, secure, and thriving in many different types of healthy relationships. I could taste, see, hear, and feel who I was becoming as a woman, waking up the infinite potential me that I could become.

Ten months later, on a beautiful autumn day, I was hiking in Oak Creek Canyon near Sedona to reflect on a particularly profound, transformational ceremonial experience following a thirteen-day healing ceremony. I sat on a big rock in the middle of the creek, looking at the brilliant fall leaves and listening to the musical flow of the water over the rocks. In that moment, time stopped. I felt altered, as if I was in a dream.

A huge monarch butterfly landed on my rock. I heard a clear voice ask me, "Are you willing to bring 144,000 Rainbow Light Warriors to the light?" As a person who always says yes, of course I said, "Yes." I got up, realizing in that moment what I had said yes to...

I took this experience back to my teacher, who affirmed I had been called to take the teachings of this very ancient shamanic lineage out into the world. A Rainbow Light Warrior is someone who does battle with their inner darkness so they can shine their light more brightly out into the world. When we bring our shining light out into the world as our gifts, we are part of the solution to heal our brothers and sisters and restore balance and harmony on Grandmother Earth.

The children of Grandmother Earth are not only the people, but also the rocks, plants, animals and all life on Grandmother Earth. In this book you will read about the conflict of inner darkness and the awareness of inner light. What I'm referring to is character refinement and healing in terms of cleaning up our shame, self-pity, negative habits and thoughts so we can serve the Light as a shiny, sacred human being through the expression of our true nature, our gifts, and our most authentic wise self.

It is my desire to offer you the wisdom of my journey with stress so you can gain a nugget or two that will empower you to put your shining light out into the world, to shine your light brightly in your uniquely authentic way and make a ripple, like a pebble cast into a pond.

At the time I sat on the rock and said yes, I was too naïve to fully comprehend what I was saying yes to. I look back on that moment and can see that I was very receptive to Spirit talking to me through nature that day. That calling still lives within me and reminds me to keep going, to share my message that supports people to wake-up consciously so they can access more self-awareness and choose to step out of their habits, thoughts and patterns that keep them stuck in their shadow so they may take a stand to shine brighter with their light. Ironically, a part of me always had an awareness of my calling, but I had the perception that I would be a nun or serve through the

Catholic Church in some way. Catholicism was not my calling after all, but it prepared me for who I am growing into.

Following my calling on the banks of Oak Creek, I apprenticed to a very ancient, shamanic lineage in October 2003, a lineage derived from medicine men and women, and shamans, of the indigenous peoples of Turtle Island (what is now North, Central and South America). The indigenous people, before the formalized tribes that we know today, were very wise in the ways of Grandmother Earth and the Universe, or the "As Above," meaning all that is spirit, and "So Below," meaning all that is in physical form on the earth. The wisdom from the different tribes was woven together like a braid of hair into this oral tradition. This is called a "Twisted Hair" tradition because the knowledge and wisdom is not from one particular tribe, but from many of the early earth cultures.

The lineage I study founded the first wisdom school in 1254 BC. The shamans who carried the knowledge out to the tribes can be depicted with their hair braided into a knot that sits on the front of their head, just above their forehead. As an oral tradition, there is little that can be "Googled." Over time, this knowledge worked and evolved with the people who used it. Ultimately, this ancient shamanic path is a wisdom school for personal evolution through self-discovery and character refinement. It consists of fifteen gateways, or levels of highly transformational ceremonies, and teachings that guide one along a spiritual path towards enlightenment.

Shamanism is an interesting word these days. It brings up all sorts of assumptions about plant journeys, of altered states of consciousness induced from ingestion of various forms of plants such as San Pedro, Peyote or Ayahuasca. Currently, there is a popular trend to find someone who identifies as a shaman, or to travel to a faraway place such as Peru to experience such a plant journey with a Peruvian shaman. Ingesting these plant medicines may lead to an expansive experience for some beyond a recreational intent, but the plants alone are not shamanism. The plant world is only one of Grandmother Earth's worlds. For example, there is the mineral world, animal world, human world, and the spirit world. If you only factor in the plant, you are lacking all the other parts of creation.

Shamanism uses the term "Medicine" often in terms of the natural gift or essence of something. My spiritual path is a Medicine Path because it brings self-healing, and we often refer to our spiritual community as "The Medicine." We refer to each other within our community as our medicine brothers and sisters. In shamanic traditions, a person's medicine is their talents, skills, and abilities. It is their gift or way to bring healing to self, life and others. For example, my medicine is that I help heal the hearts of others. Ironically, I was a cardiac nurse for many years, and it is only recently that I can see that in the work I do to support my clients there is always the tenderness of healing the broken heart. It's not always about a relationship that ended, but is more often tied to the many key emotional events over a lifetime that are heartbreaking to the spirit of a person.

For me, it was not such a stretch to go from practicing Catholicism to shamanism. Shamanism is not a religion. It is a spiritual path for self-growth and healing through self-exploration and engagement with teachings to learn ancient wisdom taught through a circular thinking process called Medicine Wheels. The wisdom is then applied to ceremonial experiences to integrate the teachings deeply and connect us to Spirit through nature and all aspects of creation which leads to illuminations to know ourselves better.

As the path I have chosen to grow with, or what I call my path with heart, the Sweet Medicine SunDance Path awakened me as a Spiritual Warrior. A Spiritual Warrior is someone who takes a stand for their light and dedicates oneself to a path of continual evolutionary growth, through acquisition of knowledge and wisdom to catalyze self-growth and become part of the solution for change on the planet. My spiritual path offers expansive teachings and ceremonial experiences that support self-healing of my past pain stories, to transform poor patterns into more productive patterns and raise my conscious awareness so I can exercise my free will muscle, and so much more than I can share in this writing.

The Medicine Wheels and keys of knowledge unlock the mystery of our Soul. Shamanism explores the interconnection of all forms of all things in the Universe. It connects the world of Spirit to the physical world and gives context to how we are a spiritual being having a human-being experience in our lifetime. Shamanism uses a combination of ancient wisdom and alchemical ceremonial experiences to create a deep, rapid transformation of self-growth and character refinement. When I use the terms alchemical ritual or ceremony, I'm referring to how the powers of nature are used following specific steps, like following a recipe, that restores beauty, balance, and harmony within a ceremonial context. Shamanism uses nature for connection and healing of the five aspects of being human: emotional, physical, mental, spiritual, and sexual. The shamanic lineage I am apprenticed to is a rigorous path of Spiritual Warriors and a strong dedication within my lifestyle.

My ceremonial experiences are profound and diverse, more than I can begin to describe here as an expression of mysticism. In my lineage we say we "Source the force of the Everything." This is the potential to direct where the flow of energy can go to create a shift, a power, or an outcome for transformation. "The Everything" includes all of creation. When Jesus performed his miracles, he was harnessing the powers in nature to create magic. We may feel faith for what Jesus did when he performed miracles without questioning how it was possible, but we don't always appreciate how magical Jesus was when he did those amazing miracles, including his resurrection. Shamanism gave me a profound understanding for who Jesus was and how he performed his miracles by accessing the powers of creation.

At the core of alchemy is male-female balance. In nature, the energy of masculine and feminine is always balanced. As humans, we get these energies out of balance for many reasons. Often, when we are stressed out and in resistance we are out of male-female balance. The feminine principle is receptive and creative energy: think of women conceiving and giving birth. The masculine principle is active and conceptive: think about how men are focused on taking direct action from A to B to gain a solution. We each have both aspects of feminine and masculine principles within us. Feminine energy brings beauty and masculine energy brings blessings. Both are equally essential to bring balance, and yet we can appreciate the different nature of each principle. My spiritual path has helped me rebalance the feminine and masculine energies within myself as essential to access my healed self.

Reflecting over the years since I committed to this path, it is my surprise that I have wandered from my practice of formalized religion. I still enjoy the Catholic ways that I share with my family and still step into many of my Catholic traditions, but the way I connect to God now is much deeper and more personal, like a true relationship. I am able to experience Great Spirit, or God, and the mystery of the Holy Spirit in all of creation. I would say that shamanism expanded my view of spirituality and deepened my connection and faith.

There are many similarities of the rituals practiced in church with the rituals I practice within my Shamanic Path. I understand many of the rituals I followed as a Catholic now with a deeper understanding of what I was doing or creating by following the ways of the Church. As you enter a Catholic church, you bless yourself with the element of holy water in the sign of the cross. In my shamanic tradition, water is life and symbolizes the stream of livingness, and making the sign of the cross honors the four directions on your physical body.

When you enter a pew at church you genuflect, or bow, to honor the presence of Spirit on the altar. When I enter a purification lodge to pray, I bow and honor "all my relations" as I enter the lodge space at the doorway. Priests use incense at times during certain celebrations. They burn incense in a burner and waft the smoke in a specific pattern of the four directions as part of ceremonial ritual. In shamanism we use an herbal mixture called smudge. Smudging is the process of lighting dried herbs and wafting the smoke around our physical body or into a space. I smudge my aura any time I want to step into a state of presence and connection to energies within a space, as well as restore male-female balance when I smudge from left to right and up the midline of my body with the feather fan. To smudge, I use an herbal mixture made up of sage, cedar and lavender to banish negative energy and bring balance and beauty. Sweetgrass is sometimes added to bring blessings. Cleansing my energy with smudge is like bathing my body and aura with positive energy.

Another example of the parallels I have experienced relates to the Catholic Sacrament of Reconciliation, also referred to as confession. Similarly in Shamanism, when we pray in ceremony, we do a "give-away." A give-away prayer is spoken to release the specific negative habits, behaviors, or thinking that block us from our shining are something to give-away. It may be a give-away of procrastination, doubt, fear, or any of the negativity that motivates us to not be our most authentic self. Give-aways often relate to those aspects of our character refinement we want to heal to improve our character.

Many people today seek spiritual connection beyond their traditional religious practices, drifting away from the formalized way of practicing faith and seeking new ways to experience spirituality. When we are part of a church or religious community, we come together to pray with other like-minded individuals. Even the most faithful will need to cultivate an individual connection with something greater, such as God or Spirit, and to bring that personal connection into our day-to-day life beyond the church service. Spiritual connection can be experienced in many ways within, or separate from, a traditional faith practice.

A sense of belonging to community is a great resource for stress resilience and it is equally beneficial when we can make that connection to something greater than ourselves to lean into. Spiritual connection and practices are essential elements of stress resilience in whatever form they take when they provide a platform for personal growth and hope.

Just as I crossed the bridge between Catholicism and shamanism, I have also integrated Western medicine with shamanic healing. Many people bash Western medicine today, but I have found that we need it for diagnosis, and at times, treatments. For example, if we break our leg or have a clogged heart artery, we need the technology, tools and physical assessment skills of Western medicine to accurately diagnose the problem. We may need a procedure, surgery or medication to manage the symptoms. Often, Western medicine is the bridge to greater healing.

When I had asthma, I was dependent on multiple inhalers, peak flow meter readings, tablets and bouts of steroids. I needed the treatment to manage my symptoms as I healed, but it was all the other things I did to change my life and lifestyle through self-exploration and mind-body-spirit experiences that brought healing and freed me from the need of any medications. Today, I live completely free of any signs or symptoms of asthma. When I was diagnosed, my doctor told me I would always have asthma symptoms. What if I had taken his word for it and not explored avenues for healing? I would be living a different story today.

I went through many months of diagnosis and treatment to detox my system and boost my immune system. On the other side of my intensive healing, I am a changed person. There was a turning point when I experienced a much stronger state of health, and over time, as I continued to do my inner work, all the symptoms completely resolved. My healing journey continued to evolve once I started on the path of my shamanic studies to heal in mind-body-spirit layer by layer.

In my case, I needed the Western medicine physician who specialized in training in environmental medicine to address my issues. I needed the diagnostic tools, the prescribed interventions and the supplements and dietary changes. What really kicked up the healing process were all the other things I did to heal my heart, to feel more self-acceptance, and to gain a stronger connection through my spiritual practices, including healing through ceremonial experiences where I was able to drop deeply into my inner landscape to heal those formerly hidden parts of myself.

CHAPTER 4: FOUNDATIONAL STRESS MASTERY PRACTICES AND TOOLS

"Mindfulness: Paying attention to the present moment with intention, while letting go of judgment as if your life depends on it."

Dr. Jon Kabat-Zinn

A core skill for stress resilience is your capacity to stay in the present moment with self-awareness. It's essential to center ourselves and stay focused in the present so we can increase our mindful awareness, "the awareness that arises from paying attention, on purpose, in the present moment and non-judgmentally," (Jon Kabat-Zinn, *Full Catastrophe Living*).

This attitude of being in the present and centered, non-judgmentally, within our core is a skill to practice. Doing a formal mindful awareness practice is one way to train the muscle to be more present and aware in the moment through mindful awareness. The test comes when we can keep our attention in the present moment in our day-to-day living, not only during those times we are sitting in a formal practice.

The concept of dropping into our core, or into our center, is where we can get out of our busy analytical mind and listen from an embodied place in our heart, womb, or gut. Many live life between their chin and their eyebrows, relying completely on their intellect to "smart" their way through life. This approach requires individuals to rely on their mental capacity to analyze and think through their stress triggers, which can induce anxiety and reactivity, and feel exhausting.

When we take a deep breath and drop our attention down into our heart, or into our internal center of gravity (located 2-3 finger breadths below our naval and back a bit towards our spine), we can listen to our womb, or dantian, or for the brothers, to our gut. Remember the expression "trust your gut" or "listen to your intuition?"

> From this centered place, we can access our
> inner intuition and wisdom to creatively
> problem solve or otherwise respond with an
> attitude of resilience.

Taking a deep breath into our center ignites the parasympathetic nervous system for the natural stress resilience mode called *rest and digest* so we can access the meet-the-challenge stress response. When we react from a purely mental place, we risk triggering the sympathetic nervous system, opening the flood gate to the fight-or-flight stress response. When we can hold the state of mindful awareness as an attitude, or as a skill that we train into, we can respond when stress triggers hit and stay out of reactivity and energy loss.

Mindfulness, or as referred to in this work, mindful awareness, is paying attention to what really matters in the moment without getting caught in the inner dialogue. Maybe you've seen the cartoon of the adult walking beside a child outdoors. The adult cartoon head bubble is full of mental words, pictures and has lots going on. The head bubble of the child shows a flower, or the sun only, in the spaciousness of the bubble. The point of the cartoon for mindful awareness is that the child's empty head bubble is not better than the adult's full mind. Mindful awareness says that you simply notice from a neutral place, without judgment, that you have a lot going on in your mind. It's naming what you notice for yourself, without judgment or a charge around it, that is key. Mindful awareness is at the heart of stress resilience so we can pay attention to behaviors we indulge in when stressed or in a resistance pattern, and instead choose an action that will empower us to respond to the situation more productively, rather than destructively.

When we are single-focused and not multi-tasking, we can be more consciously aware so can tune into our feelings, thoughts and words.

> It doesn't matter if we are talking with another
> person or folding laundry — we are mindful
> when we pay attention to and connect with what
> we are experiencing in that moment.

We are awake and not numbed out, distracted, or asleep. We can be mindful during exercise or doing simple movement when we focus on that exact activity of movement. We can use mindful awareness to appreciate our food when we eat if we really taste it with palate gratification, smelling our food, taking in its visual beauty and feeling the gratitude for the many hands that touched our food along the way to make it possible for it to be on our plate. We can connect with gratitude for the plant or animal that gave its life so that we may live. Yes, even our veggies give up their lives so that we may live as we eat them for their nutritional giveaway. In nature there is a natural cycle of death that brings life, as we can see in the decaying tree that is home to the insects that are eaten by the critters as part of the death bringing life cycle. The food we eat is part of this cycle, thus we can be aware of our interconnection with nature through our food.

When we multitask, we are distracting ourselves. For example, when we're on our cell phone, reading or watching TV while eating a meal, we are not connecting to our food or appreciating how our food is nourishing us with savory pleasure. Emotional eating is a common distraction response for stress or resistance, where we may not even notice what is going into our mouth. If we are not paying attention while we eat, we may inhale our food without fully tasting it, experiencing the deliciousness of it, nor sensing when we are full.

Mindful awareness is not tunnel vision or a narrow focus. When we focus on what really matters in the moment, or simply notice what is coming up for us, we can take a pause to focus and appreciate what is around us. We can open up our point of view with mental receptivity to notice and experience more of what is in the present moment in greater detail. Paradoxically, when we eliminate distractions around us, or simply notice the distractions, a bigger space opens within us to explore new perspectives. Where we choose to place our attention is what grows, either positive or negative, in the principle of Attention = Power.

The mind is never "empty," but in the internal
stillness, we can stay focused with a quiet,
curious mind that is open and receptive,
without distractions from the inner critic or
stress dialogue loop that can occupy a busy,
over-analytical mind.

It's quiet in terms of the inner dialogue and the external distractions in our environment. When we hit a zone of awareness we can experience timelessness, yet sometimes what we notice when we simply pay attention is how busy our mind is with the clutter of distracting thoughts. The key is to notice whatever is in our mind without any judgment, good or bad, but allowing whatever is there to just be. This is the skill of presence.

Mindfulness practices are often taught by trained mindfulness practitioners. The practices I offer are designed to cultivate mindful moments using centering practices with focused breathing. There are purists who will distinguish the difference between mindfulness and mindful awareness or centering. In this work, I use the term mindfulness and mindful awareness interchangeably, as defined by Dr. Jon Kabat-Zinn. Mindful awareness in this context helps us to be able to respond with self-awareness when a stress trigger hits and to stay out of reactivity.

Mindful awareness helps us to access a stress-resilient state or attitude, and there are multiple ways to access awareness in the moment. It doesn't necessarily mean we are sitting in lotus position or meditating in the corner with incense burning. We can experience mindful awareness in any of the activities we love that put us into the "zone of awareness." The activities that quiet our mind and pull us into a single focus are when we feel timeless. Remember the expression "time flies when you're having fun?" We can access mindful awareness while engaging in a hobby, a creative project, or while fishing or hiking in nature. Even pausing to gaze at a sunset can bring us into the present moment.

The more ways we access mindful moments through periods of single focus with no distractions, the more we can cross-train being more present throughout our day. With consistent practice, when the stress triggers hit we can pause, take a breath to drop down into our center and respond to the situation creatively, intuitively, and neutrally to feel more emotionally balanced and less reactive. One of the main benefits of mindful awareness "practices" is exactly that – *to practice being mindful* in the moments we are tested and challenged with stress triggers.

Practice: 4-7-8 Breath to Stop the Inner Dialogue

The 4-7-8 Centering Breath Technique comes from Andrew Weil, MD from the Arizona Center for Integrative Medicine. It is simple to access because you can do it anywhere, in any situation. You can even do it while you drive, but don't close your eyes! While you are simultaneously counting and breathing you cannot maintain the inner dialogue in your head.

As you connect to your breath deeply you are becoming more grounded and more connected to the present moment:

- Breathe in deeply through your nose as you count to 4.
- Hold your breath for a count of 7.
- Exhale the breath for a count of 8.
- Repeat the cycle 3-4 more times.

Putting your focus on your core as you inhale deeply will create more presence, balance the emotions, and allow access to the intuitive/ instinctual channel for deeper listening and enhanced creative problem solving.

This simple technique is an excellent way to rebalance if you've just had a blow up with someone and you want to regain your emotional balance, or if you are preparing to have an important conversation. If you are impacted by anxiety, this technique can help you to get out of the fight-or-flight loop and into the parasympathetic mode to access resiliency through the meet-the-challenge stress response.

Practice: The Core of the Matter – One-point, Power Place and Dantian

Speaking of the core, this is the sweet spot located at your center of gravity that is a built-in empowerment center as part of our human design. This power place is an essential key to presence, physical grounding and emotional balance. I've worked with different teachers who call this center of gravity by different names, including the one-point, womb space, power place and dantian, but the benefits are universal.

> Wikipedia: Dantian, dan t'ian, dan tien or tan t'ien is loosely translated as "elixir field," "sea of qi," or simply "energy center." Dantian are the Qi Focus Flow Centers, important focal points for meditative and exercise techniques such as qigong, martial arts such as t'ai chi ch'uan, and in traditional Chinese medicine.

What's important is where this place is located inside our physical body. You will find it 2-3 finger breadths below your naval and a few inches inwards from the naval, back towards your spine. Energetically it is between the second and third chakra. For women, it is where the physical womb is located. When we place our attention on this power place we can embody more presence, allowing us to feel more mentally and emotionally neutral and grounded. This opens the door to creative problem solving and turns up the volume of our wise intuitive voice to meet challenging situations with confidence and clarity. Placing our awareness into our one-point or womb space/dantian at our core will support stress resilience and calm our inner dialogue related to the inner mental and emotional roller coaster.

To maximize the benefits of this powerful center, create a regular practice of being home — home in your body, and home in your presence, with stability that is anchored in this space. A regular practice of centering into our power place makes us more magnetic to others because they can feel our presence physically in the space. The practice supports us to keep our heart open as we engage with others, especially when we're feeling vulnerable. We can enhance our listening beyond our physical ears when we listen from our one-point or womb/dantian space.

Practice: Technique to Practice Being "Home" in Your One-point
You want to be home in your one-point often throughout your day. You can shift your awareness to your one-point with every new space you enter and during every important conversation. You can ask yourself "Am I home?" and place your attention into your power place. It will feel like a reboot of your focus.

- Inhale deeply and drop your awareness down to that place 2-3 finger breadths below the naval and back towards the spine. (This is your physical center of gravity, as is experienced by many athletes.)
- Use your imagination to anchor your awareness into that power place by imagining there's a crystal in the center of your one-point.
- Or you might imagine a glowing ember of magma sitting in this power place that lights up with every deep inhale of your breath.

This practice is energy conserving as well as grounding you in presence. It also opens access to the focus of *Attention = Power,* which states that where your attention goes is what grows. Placing attention into your one-point or your core will support you to be present, magnetic and non-judgmental to meet any challenge with a resilient attitude. This supports deeper listening so you can hold space for another.

Practice: 4-7-8 Breath with One-point

When you practice the 4-7-8 breath, combine the techniques of breathing into your one-point when you inhale for a count of 4 down into your power place.

CHAPTER 5: TYRANT TRIGGERS

*"When we are no longer able to change
a situation, we are challenged to change
ourselves."*

Viktor E. Frankl

It was dinner time on the ranch one summer. I was four years old. All seven ranch kids sat at the long table eating our dinner. Stormy, our babysitter, was in charge while all the parents were in town. The dinner table was noisy with a lot of laughing, for everyone except me. I was in tears as Stormy was teasing me and saying things that made me cry even harder, then pointed out I was "crying like a baby." She then tried to cajole me to stop crying and offered me some Coca-Cola. Handing me the dixie cup, she said I had to drink it all. As I took a sip, my crying was renewed — she had heavily salted it. As I made a face, she sternly said I had to finish it. My reaction made the other kids break into gales of laughter, all except my cousin Charlie, who was my age. He quietly sat in his own world, neither laughing nor paying attention to my plight.

Next, Stormy brought out a cracked mirror. She held it up in front of me and told me my face was so ugly from crying that I broke her mirror. I sat there miserable and crying for the duration of dinner. I never spoke up for myself. I never left the table. None of the other kids, including my brothers, stood up for me. My parents returned home later and not one word was spoken about the incident.

When I was five, my mother took me into her bedroom to show me the Dresden-blue velour shirt she had purchased for me at a rummage sale. She was excited about it and eager for me to try it on. I pulled it over my head and told her it felt hot, scratchy, and tight around my neck. She instantly became furious and grabbed the shirt from me, slammed it back into her dresser drawer and said to me, using a tone and words I will never forget, "You are a spoiled rotten brat. I will never buy you another thing as long as you live!" I quietly stood there beside her dresser, feeling completely ashamed and unlovable. We never spoke about the shirt again and I never saw it again.

Another incident happened one day when a new babysitter walked up the long driveway. Around 1965, when the style was for poufy, back-combed hair with big, flipped curls and "mod" or wild, psychedelic-colored clothes, my babysitter walked up the driveway with her platinum blonde "big" hairdo, dangly earrings, bright lipstick and wearing a bright, swishy bell-bottomed pant suit. She had a swing in her step and a smile on her face. Standing by the door, watching her come closer, I felt excited that she was going to be my babysitter and greeted her with, "Hi! You look sexy!" I was clear in my choice of the word "sexy," because to me, she looked like a beautiful movie star, and I thought sexy was a term to describe the fashion that famous movie stars adopted.

Hearing my words, my mother grabbed me by that tender upper arm spot, dragged me to the bathroom and washed my mouth out with soap. I was in big trouble, and I took the punishment without speaking my case or standing up for myself. I was clear that I had done something very wrong, even though I knew my intent was not naughty. I felt guilty and ashamed. The soap washed the joy right out of me. Mother made me apologize to the Babysitter for my rudeness.

My best friend lived across the alley and was someone I played with daily during the school year. She had a very creative imagination and thought up fun make-believe games. She made the rules, and I followed them, with her always playing the dominant figure while I was the subservient participant. She seemed to always play the smarter older sister, the teacher or the mother. If we played "boy island" she was just a little prettier than me, or her boyfriend was more handsome than mine. When we played mermaids, her scales were more beautiful than mine and her hair was longer with more sparkles as we ran around the yard, pretending we were mermaids swimming in the ocean. One day, I spoke up while we played dress-up, asking if I could wear the blue costume instead of the orange one this time. There were tears over that request. Her mom came into the room and called me a spoiled rotten brat, then sent me home. Feeling unworthy, guilty, and at fault for the fight, I sobbed as I ran across the alley back home.

Sometime later, we made up and returned to our wildly imaginative make-believe games. I never spoke up again to ask for what I wanted, but always allowed her to dominate the roles and set the rules while I followed her lead. She was what is referred to as a Lord Queen Tyrant. This form of tyrant would later show up for me in the form of authority figures. Much later, I would learn how to speak up and take a stand for my case to meet this flavor of tyrant.

Growing up on the ranch every summer with my two brothers and the other older kids, I was constantly teased to tears. They took delight in tormenting me in that way. When sobbing, I was not comforted when the adults advised, "If you stop reacting to their teasing they will stop." What I heard when they said this, was the bullying was my fault and I was the one who was in control of making it stop. I was never able to change my attitude or my approach with older kids to get a different response. Paradoxically, I turned myself inside out and practically did summersaults to win their friendly attention and feel included by them. This would open the door to more teasing and torment, so the cycle of emotional wounding perpetuated. I lived inside the cycle of my insecurity and lack of self-confidence to continuously seek their approval so I could feel loved and liked and be included. Eventually, as my brothers matured, they stopped teasing me and peace was restored.

> I carried this approval-seeking pattern into my
> adult years, only it wasn't the teasing bullies
> who tormented me, but the authority figures
> with whom I worked.

For a significant portion of my adult years, I was triggered into stress by all authority figures, including bosses, managers and doctors who intimidated me professionally as a nurse, and later, while working with leadership in my various roles. In the era of my nursing career, it was not unusual for physicians to take out their frustration on the nurses who cared for their patients. I got rattled and lost my space easily, which induced instant stress feelings of doubt and insecurity. When I felt like this on the job, I made mistakes, or worse, did not speak up to ask clarifying questions regarding my patients' care. I would do anything to not have to call a doctor for orders if I could have someone else make the call. The inner critic voice was very loud when dealing with anyone of perceived authority over me. I gave away my power through apology in those situations, rather than taking a stand for myself. It was a very disempowering pattern and created the energetic that I wanted to disappear rather than be visible, not wanting to be seen or noticed.

We get triggered into stress by those people and situations in our lives that "tyrant" us. Other names for tyrants are bullies, persecutors, or controllers. These are the difficult people or situations that push our buttons, setting off an emotional charge that triggers insecurity, doubt, annoyance, blame, shame, and guilt — any of which can result in disempowerment and energy loss. Mastering tyrants can provide a way to stay neutral, focused, and maintain our energy and not get pulled into their drama and pain game when tyrants do what they do to poke at us.

When we allow ourselves to be impacted by time and space, as well as the behavior and words of those in our everyday life, we will feel energy loss and emotional turbulence from our reaction to any form of these tyrants. Internally, we feel highly reactive. Externally, we either shrink to disappear, rather than stand up for ourselves, or become highly reactive and emotionally charged.

Getting our buttons pushed by a tyrant comes in many forms. When we are not centered and react, the result is that we lose our space internally. Feeling tyranted by certain individuals can feel like being micromanaged, manipulated, criticized, or can be someone who has a behavior or communication style that perpetually annoys us. Tyrants can cause us to feel small irritating annoyances, as well as the big ones that put us on edge, shake our confidence or throw off our emotional balance. Time can be a tyrant if we are constantly fighting against time in our day to fit everything in.

Often, the individuals and situations that tyrant us are those events and people over which we have no control. They are not going to change, so it is in our circle to change how we engage with them. One thing we can do is shift our attitude by changing our perspective of how we think about the tyrant. We can also change our engagement by shifting our approach or behavior in how we are dealing with the person or situation. For example, let's say you planned a reunion picnic and it's raining on the day of the event. You can't control the fact that it's raining, but you can adjust your attitude from being negative or disappointed to finding a solution-oriented plan for the reunion to move ahead. The new attitude is to stay open to how the gathering can come together for everyone to connect, and the new approach is to find an alternative location for the gathering to take place without the impact of rain. Alternatively, you might find a way to align with the rain, such as inviting everyone to bring an umbrella and rain gear.

Some tyrants are not related strictly to a "no control" situation, but relate to poor behavior, bad habits or disempowering communication that hit our self-confidence and self-worth. When we learn how to close the door to a tyrant, we will feel unshakable in our inner security and outer confidence, able to stay calm and neutral in the face of the tyrant.

> Closing the door on a tyrant is called "counting coup," and we will always gain an increased measure of self-worth when we are successful in the process of counting coup.

When we recognize that someone is a bully, button pusher or major stress trigger in our life, we can stop the torment by learning how to close the door *on the effect* of the bad behavior or annoying pattern. In my practice, we work with our "Tyrant Teachers" as an opportunity to gain learning from the situation and stop the energy loss from the emotional hit.

> Our tyrants will never change their behavior
> until we change our response.

Where we do have control is in our response to our tyrants and this is a hidden opportunity for personal growth and character refinement. What our tyrants teach us is an insight about *our own* insecurity, vulnerability, or shadow behavior. When we experience dysfunctional behaviors or habits in others, many times we will uncover that we also have a similar shadow trait within ourselves. This is the surprise about tyrants — it is *our own inner tyrant* that will open the door to the outer tyrant. What we see as annoying or disruptive in others tells us about what we also have as a hidden behavior or pattern within ourselves. *This is why there is such a gift when we are open to what we can learn about ourselves from our Tyrant Teachers.*

Our tyrants unconsciously offer us a teaching, providing a glimpse of our own internal shadow. When we see a truth through self-awareness, we have the ability to change our perspective, and once we get the lesson, we will be able to stop reacting and feel more neutral so we can close the door to that tyrant trigger.

From my experience, the real victory happens when I have the courage and honesty to speak up and confront the tyrant with the truth of their impact on me. Once I see the truth, I can speak about what I'm experiencing with that person and close the door to their effect on me. I can then hold a neutral state with balanced emotions and the relationship instantly improves. It improves because I'm now clear about the boundaries I need to set, and they are clear about how to communicate or engage with me more authentically in a way that empowers both of us with understanding.

The flip side is that if I never speak up and confront the truth of what I learned about myself, or what I am experiencing when engaging with the other, the triggering behavior, energy loss and emotional reactivity will continue. And if I don't speak up, and name the truth of what I now see, the other person will not have the benefit of gaining awareness for themselves, so will stay in their shadow or triggering/ annoying behavior without any opportunity to rise above to a new level of engagement with others.

> **The greatest gift of "counting coup" on a tyrant is that both win. There is no "I win, you lose." When we find the courage to address our tyrannical relationships openly and honestly, addressing these difficult relationships from a win-win perspective rather than a blame and fault-finding conversation, we will always empower a stronger, more respectful connection.**

It's worth the investment of energy conservation and inner peace to have that heart-to-heart with those difficult people. In my case it was authority figures, bosses, leaders, teachers, brothers, parents, friends' parents etc., that triggered my inner shadow of doubt and insecurity.

Insecurity was behind the veil of nearly all my stress patterns triggered by these authority figures.

Turning around my insecurity with authority figures has been very empowering and enabled healing from my old pain stories. Each conversation that happened was a conscious act of bravery on my part, to assert myself and take control of my own need for inner peace. What I learned about closing the door on tyrants is broken down into a six-step process. Ultimately, the goal of closing the door on any tyrant in our life can result in a gain of awareness for both parties. If no one ever speaks up to name the specific dynamic with honesty, or confront with kindness about their behavior or impact towards others, the tyrant will continue their poor behavior, remaining unconscious of their impact on others with a lack of self-awareness. When we can have a heart-to-heart honest conversation, they will have the *opportunity to choose* to make a change or to grow in some way. We are offering a gift of self-awareness to them.

As a little girl, had I had the maturity to handle my brothers' teasing this way, I may have stopped the torment much sooner. This is what adults meant when they said that if I stopped reacting to their teasing, my brothers and the older kids would no longer gain pleasure from dominating me and would turn their attention elsewhere.

There are six steps to assert self-authority to resolve the inner conflict with our tyrants.

1. For a tyrant to impact us negatively, we have already been our own internal tyrant. We open the door to the outer tyrant from our own inner dialogue around our insecurities or shadow patterns.
    You can ask yourself "How this person is actually a mirror

of some insecurity within myself?" Be curious about what feelings are being triggered internally.

For example, if we are repulsed by and judgmental towards someone we consider a hoarder, what part of us is aligned with the energetic of hoarding or clutter? Many times, what repulses us, irritates us or triggers our insecurity is in fact some similar energetic, fear or shadow behavior we have internally that we would not normally see or want others to see. It's a blind spot because it is often in our unconscious.

2. Once we can see why this person is able to push our buttons from our internal tyrant, we have an awareness of how this person causes us to lose our calm and energy when they poke at us. It may feel like a power struggle. Often, we can see their insecurity as they attempt to stay in control over us. This is true for those who trigger shame, guilt, and self-pity in us as well.

3. Once we have the awareness of our internal programming, we can see their weakness. We can separate what is our issue from what is their stuff. We can close the door on the tyrant when we realize that their behavior is really about them, not us. This is a key step – when we are able to stop taking ownership of what they are trying to put on us.

4. Once we're able to stay neutral and remember that it's not really about us – it's about their own insecurity or other internal block, we can stop the energy drain and let their behavior or words bounce right off. We have created a boundary or bottom line between what is our energy and what is theirs.

5. Once we stop "dancing the dance" with them by not reacting to their behavior, the relationship will change. They will either stop or turn their attention to someone else. We do this when we take responsibility to engage differently.

   When we change, the relationship changes without waiting for that person or situation to change. The tyrant behavior won't change until we show up to the engagement differently. When we take responsibility to change our attitude about it or change our engagement with it, we stop dancing this dance. Thus the tyrant has lost their hold on us and we have stopped giving away our power. The outcome of this is a strengthened relationship, especially if we can have a heart-to-heart conversation with the person we perceive is our tyrant.

6. To really close the door, we can offer a neutral reflection back to that person, delivered not from blame or reactivity, but from a place of a personal boundary. Placing a boundary or bottom line will help us to take the higher road of maturity and awareness. Many times, our tyrants are unaware of the power game they play against others. We can offer a nonjudgmental reflection to our tyrant, using a neutral tone, which may sound like this: "When you say xyz to me..." or "I hear you say...." or "When you use that tone of xyz..." You can use this reflection format to name or highlight a specific behavior as well. With the right reflection offered back, enacting a boundary, or making an agreement around the rules of engagement, we are offering the gift of awareness about the impact of their

behavior so we can both learn from the engagement as a win-win.

For example, if you know someone who has the habit of always borrowing things without returning them, you might say, "You may borrow my stapler, but I want it returned to my desk by the end of today with staples loaded and in working order."

Another example is to address how you respond when someone is highly critical or negative towards you. You can ask, "Will you rephrase that? I can't take in your feedback when you speak to me like that." Or "When you interrupt my focus at work, I lose my flow. Is there a time that we can schedule this conversation so I can really focus on what you have to say?"

I once had a teacher yell at me in an outburst of feedback that made me completely shut down. An energetic wall came up as my self-defense, so all her words bounced off. I could not receive a single word of her feedback. I couldn't hear her words. Afterwards, I felt full of shame and despondence.

A week later, I met with her again and told her that when she communicated to me like that I shut down from the fight-or-flight response and was unable to take in or hear her words. My boundary, or bottom line, was to let her know how to communicate with me so I can take in her feedback and be receptive to what I need to learn. I could not hear her words because I felt personally under attack and criticized, even if what she said was true. I was triggered into survival mode. Now that we have a clear agreement on how to offer feedback in a way that I can hear it, our relationship is on a new level of mutual respect and understanding. I felt the energy gain of empowerment when I spoke up for what I needed from her in order for me to be receptive to learning.

If no one is willing to confront poor behavior or challenge communication by bringing awareness to it, the perceived persecutor may never have the opportunity to see how their negative pattern impacts others, and thus choose a new way. They will stay asleep if we don't speak up. We are actually providing the opportunity for them to become more self-aware when we find the courage to confront their behavior. Speaking up can make difficult relationships shift with mutual understanding.

> Ultimately, nothing will change – for us or the tyrant – until one or both gain awareness of the dynamic and takes responsibility for behavior change.

We each take responsibility for what is ours alone, and not the other person's. This may look like agreements, boundaries or acceptance with awareness, but we can only take responsibility for ourselves as we have no control over their decision to change or not. What I learned for myself, for example, is that it is my responsibility to let anyone offering me feedback know to ask my permission first, otherwise I will shut down, receiving the feedback as criticism, if I can hear it at all.

> When we successfully turn tyranting behavior around by confronting or facing the problem, we will increase our self-measure, which then quiets the inner tyrant who opened the door in the first place.

This is how we "count coup" on the tyrant's ability to trigger us. Now if they do their triggering behavior, we can stay neutral, calm, and be clear about what is within our scope of responsibility. This makes us unshakable and more confident to hold our space and not take on what is not ours. This is creating a healthy boundary. This act of bravery is what empowers us when we successfully assert ourselves with our tyrant to stop this disempowering dance.

In this way, we can feel gratitude for the character refinement and life lesson our Tyrant Teacher offered us. When we close the door to this pattern of emotional stress, we can integrate wisdom and take a stand for our self-authority and maintain our inner peace.

We can feel so much stress and resistance when we don't speak up, holding onto our thoughts, ruminating and imagining what we could/should/would say. Simply noticing when you are feeling triggered, without self-judgment, is the first step towards gaining neutrality. The skill of honest, heart-to-heart communication can turn around relationships, and it starts with skills of mindful listening and tuning in.

Finding the courage to have a candid conversation with a difficult person is the number one way to turn our challenge around to where we both understand each other more clearly. This understanding can be a win-win for both.

PRACTICE:
PAUSE-NOTICE-CHOOSE©

"Between stimulus and response there is a space. In that space is our power to choose our response. In our response lies our growth and our freedom."

Viktor E. Frankl

Any time we feel overwhelmed, triggered by someone, annoyed, judgmental, or in any way impacted by another, we can practice Pause-Notice-Choose. This is another way to access mindful awareness without going into reactivity, simply by noticing our own internal response and choosing how we will respond. Ultimately, the Pause-Notice-Choose practice can support mindful awareness so we can hold space within ourselves and for another. This practice enhances listening without judgment on the outside, even if we are feeling ruffled on the inside, simply by noticing, and then choosing how we will respond:

- **Pause:** take a breath into your one-point or center in your lower belly, 2-3 finger breadths below your naval.
- **Notice:** simply notice what is happening in your internal or external environment, without judgment or reaction. Stay neutral and simply name what is there as truth.
- **Choose:** what action can you take that will empower you to hold your space versus choosing an action that will sabotage you? Will you pause and take ten deep breaths or make a cup of tea? Or will you distract yourself with emotional eating, social media scrolling, Netflix® binging, or going into reactivity?

CHAPTER 6: TENTACLES OF CO-DEPENDENCY

"If you accept the expectations of others, then you never will change the outcome."

Michael Jordan

Checking out of AJ's grocery store with six decadent, chocolate Fairy Tale Brownies, "These are for my mother," I'd be sure to let the checkout person know. I'd go to the liquor store and purchase a gallon bottle of red wine and a carton of Virginia Slims cigarettes. I was mortified, of course, as if I was a fourteen-year-old buying condoms. I stocked up on essential supplies for my mother to keep her from driving while under the influence of alcohol and multiple prescription tranquilizers. It was a matter of keeping her safe, as well as protecting innocent people on the road.

When she called me on the phone, I'd hear the ice tinkling in her glass of Johnnie Walker Red Label and brace myself for her tyranting mood. The names she called me included "door mat" as she told me to stop being in the "poor me syndrome," as if it was some exclusive club. Then she'd start in on her apology, "It's all my fault you turned out the way you did. I've ruined you." She kept raising the bar of her expectations that I would never reach. Her standards of excellence would never be enough, even if I had reached them, because her bar was consistently telling me that what I was doing was not enough. I was too fat, too thin, my hair color was wrong – too red, too blonde, too dark, or too short. Why was I a nurse when I could be a doctor? I was never able to be what she wanted me to be, but something in me constantly strived to be excellent, to try harder to excel at everything I did so I could meet her bar.

One of her favorite family stories was to tell people the family always thought I was dumb in school. At age five I flunked out of kindergarten and needed to start over the next year, which my family poked fun at for years. The report cards at my elementary school did not reflect a specific grade but documented "Satisfactory" or "Unsatisfactory" progress. My mother frequently shared, "We always thought Sara was dumb until she went to high school and got straight As. We were really surprised because we never knew she could be so smart."

As a tiny girl, I remember being with my mother in my grandparents' swimming pool while I was just learning to swim. Mother alternately bullied and cajoled me to leave the safety of the big step and swim a few strokes towards her. Her arms stretched out, she said, "Come on! You can do this!" As I pushed off the step, flailing with my arms and legs, she began moving backward. The closer I got to her, the further back she stepped into the deeper water. I was panic-stricken, feeling like I would drown and never reach her arms. I was hysterical and she was laughing at me.

That was the nature of our relationship. I would never reach the bar of her expectations because the bar was always a moving target.

Nothing I did was ever enough. There was always more or better that I could do. To feel loved and accepted by her, I learned to stretch towards excellence. This set up my pattern at an early age of pushing and striving towards perfection, thinking I would win the approval of others if I was good enough or pushed a little harder.

I loved my mother and I wanted to be a good daughter. I now understand that in her own rage-filled way she loved me dearly and wanted me to make more of my life than she did with hers. What we shared was our broken-hearted connection that bonded us together in our mother-daughter relating. Throughout my life, I tolerated her bullying and focused on how to be a pleasing daughter, not because I'm a saint, but because I was co-dependent. Never once did I rebel. I never once said no to her. There were no boundaries or bottom lines in that relationship. I was compliant. This behavior set the tone for all my relationships going forward, especially my relationships with authority figures and intimate partners.

Months before she died, I made my peace with my mother when I sincerely acknowledged her as my greatest teacher. I thanked her and truthfully spoke my deep gratitude for her capacity to keep stretching me. This was one of the most liberating and empowering acts of my life, to verbally acknowledge her not only as my greatest tyrant, but as my strongest teacher. The woman I have become is not due to a soft, nurturing, *The Brady Bunch* sort of mother, but one who confronted me, challenged me, and always expected more from me than I thought I was capable of.

I eventually came to understand my mother's rage more clearly, and that my role as the recipient of her rage was justified in her mind – ensuring I would not end up in her shoes. She made her choice to stay married, but felt trapped in the financial security of her marriage to my father. She had no skills or means of supporting herself if she divorced him. He was a successful, highly prolific entrepreneur who gained, lost and regained fortunes. The stress of his wins and losses was hard on her, but her rage was fueled by the unspeakable truth that for most of their marriage, my father had girlfriends. They remained married and he provided very well for her, even after his death, but the price she paid for security was her nearly unmanageable anxiety, barely contained with the alcohol and prescription medications she used to repress her rage.

I can see that through the constant drive to prove my value I have achieved a very successful life. The gift from my lack of owning my value is that I have become a highly independent and success-driven person. I was motivated by a need to prove myself to myself, and to "fix" myself so I would be worthy and truly happy once I arrived at success, which I defined as a destination, not as a state of being. I have invested in myself massively and created amazing life experiences from which to evolve and grow.

The downside was that I put myself in a box of black and white thinking that limited the expression of my true creativity because my plate was constantly so full. At times, I cheated myself and cut corners on experiences because I just could not fit the fullness of the opportunity or experience onto my bandwidth. I barely celebrated my successes before I was off to the next challenge. I learned to be extremely self-reliant, at the cost of not being receptive to support from others, including my relationships with men. I was not receptive to my own talents, abilities, and success, and typically downplayed my shining and success. I hid my light to be invisible.

If I don't value myself, I'm unable to prioritize my heart's desire. That makes me vulnerable to being "other" driven, with my time and energy often leading to over-giving to others. For me, that translated into workaholism. How could I say yes to my heart's desire if I couldn't squeeze me into my priorities because my plate was so full of all the things I committed to for others? I resisted making commitments for myself because I was already spread too thin and frequently overwhelmed.

This is the dark side of the Do-Gooder Syndrome — to do so much good for others, without the bandwidth to do good for ourselves. By nature, some of us are wired to be attuned to what is needed in the space and to step in and give energy to others as a response to that need. When we are so over committed, there is a point where our giving to others becomes resentful and stress provoking rather than heartfelt.

In my case, the inability to verbally speak the word "no," to set a boundary, or make an agreement, only made it worse because as I said "yes" to the requests and opportunities of others, I succumbed as a "no" to myself in my actions and priorities. If I attempted to say no, I felt guilty, so would tend to waffle emotionally and go into my "should" mentality. Or I would be neither a yes or a no, but would not commit fully because of my "should do" attitude, instead of my "want to" attitude.

Being "other" focused blocked my capacity for being receptive to my own creativity or to give to myself what I desired most, as there was no time for me in my own life. Patterns of over-giving with no bottom lines or boundaries open the door to overwhelm, burnout, depletion and co-dependency.

How co-dependency impacted my other relationships was a recurring theme. I have never been married, because for years my co-dependent patterns sabotaged my key relationships. It wasn't that I was "bad" at relationships, because at my core I'm a very caring, kind, and giving partner. My gap was my inability to clearly communicate what I wanted and needed, or to speak up if something needed to be addressed, putting me in the dark side of complacency. My desire to always be pleasing and agreeable wore on my partner, who then took charge of the decisions as I lacked decisiveness and would go with the flow. I did not have the skill to advocate for myself. I was compliant and lacked courage to speak up for myself or make waves if I wanted something different. I continued to tolerate the conditions of the relationship with an attitude of fear to "keep the peace at any price" so my partner wouldn't leave me.

Fear of being rejected was my insecurity. As an insecure person, being single was a much safer option and less risky than exposing my heart to potential rejection from someone I cared for. As a co-dependent, the rejection came anyway, as the imbalance of giving and receiving did not nourish the relationship to thrive. Learning how to keep my giving and receiving in balance through communication that is clear and co-empowered takes self-awareness and focus to not slip into my old patterns of "peace at any price."

*

With a high value on sobriety, I use work, not substances, as my medicator to numb out and distract myself. I am a workaholic. I consider myself lucky, considering my familial addiction patterns. My parents both lived with alcohol addiction, and smoking led to my mother's death from emphysema. Being a workaholic is socially acceptable, lawful, has a low threshold of the shame trigger, and created a financially comfortable lifestyle that supports my autonomy. I work a lot. I'm offered projects and extra work because I'm dependable and competent. I will always do a good job and turn things around on time, even if I must push myself to get it done. But working long hours is not sustainable for personal relationships, unless of course you're dating a fellow workaholic, and then you hardly see each other.

My work patterns started long ago as a student toiling over schoolwork for hours to get good grades. As a nurse working shifts at the hospital, I worked every other weekend, Friday to Sunday, with twelve-hour shifts that left no social time. One year it was New Year's Eve and my boyfriend and I had plans to go out to celebrate with friends. I organized an eight-hour shift that day so I could go out and celebrate that evening. My unit was short-staffed, and my scheduled eight-hour shift turned into a twelve-hour shift. Consequently, I cancelled my plans to go out with my date. Unable to say no to my work commitment, I had no boundary or bottom line to honor agreements for myself and my personal plans, placing work priorities above my personal relationship. I was blinded by my need to rescue and enable my co-workers and the patients at the cost of my own plans for pleasure. The relationship ended shortly afterwards. The pattern of prioritizing work over quality relationship time has been a recurring theme throughout my life.

My priorities with work led to many personal sacrifices over the years that I learned to accept. Now I simply say, "I'm a working person, work is what I do." Learning how to allow myself *to be* and *not do* is still a work in progress in terms of my Soul's journey. Work is my solace and my companion. I would say that this arena is where the tentacles of co-dependency still exist. I created my own business as my way to take a stand for my autonomy, yet when the offers for projects and clients come in, I still tend to say yes and load up my plate with multiple challenging opportunities.

How easy it has been to put my personal desires and projects on the back burner until I have more time, while working on other's projects. Overcoming my own resistance, I now have found within myself the ability to say yes to complete this book, primarily because the knock of Spirit has become so loud with the urgency to share the message that is coming through me as the voice of my Soul. To share my journey with co-dependency in all its shadow and its hidden teachings as a vehicle to support my personal growth is a significant energy behind the veil of stress. This book addresses the broken heartedness at the core of co-dependency, insecurity and addiction patterns collectively masked as stress. As a former cardiac nurse, it is my calling to be a heart healer, and I can only do this as I heal my own broken heart.

To feel self-acceptance and self-love is the healing salve that can be applied only with self-awareness.

All my relationships, including personal, professional and with authority figures, turned around when I cleaned up my communication. It was my lack of communication skills that sabotaged my ability to relate with others. I have learned to speak up for myself with honesty and transparency and to keep my heart open, even when I feel vulnerable. I studied multiple communication modalities, and now intentionally focus on how to be a better communicator in my relationships. Mindful listening is my new approach which supports me to respond with stronger confidence and self-authority.

One of the key nuggets I have learned came from my mentor, Rachael Jayne Groover, who said, "Changing your mindset is not as important as changing what you focus on."

Attention = Power is how we teach it in
shamanism. Where our attention goes is what
grows. Where we place our attention and focus
is what gains in power, either in the light or the
dark, the pain or the pleasure, the success or the
loss.

Turning around a sabotaging pattern starts with a shift in our focus. The new focus is the new attitude. Changing our behavior is the new approach to turn co-dependency around. Both start with self-awareness first, then acting with self-responsibility second. For me an example of Attention = Power occurs when I have a proclivity to choose a work focus over a human being focus. There are times when I need to intentionally choose people time over work time. I step away from my desk so I can spend quality time with another person to cultivate a stronger connection and build my relationship. If I focus my attention on the person and not the work, I gain a positive boost of recharge energy from pleasure as well as a surge of oxytocin for the Tend and Befriend Response to increase my resilience (Attention = Power). If I keep my attention and energy output on constantly working, I am at risk to burn out and push myself to depletion. This is the dark side of Attention = Power because the pattern of overworking is reinforced when work holds my constant attention.

*

There is always a dark or shadow side and a light side in our reactive patterns and habits. We all have these "shadows" of our dark nature that are the patterns we picked up along our life journey to cope or survive, patterns we adapted for whatever benefit we gained from these actions. Within the pattern of co-dependence, for example, we may say that the shadow patterns relate to over-giving, micromanaging, enabling, or rescuing. Ultimately, co-dependence will sabotage our key relationships because there is an imbalance of power from the one who is giving away their power to the one who is taking or receiving it. Or said another way, if one person is doing all the giving, then they are not receiving back in a balanced way.

> The "co" in co-empowerment means there
> is a two-way channel, with both giving
> and receiving without a power struggle,
> manipulation or control.

But if we can see the light side of why someone would unconsciously pick up the pattern of co-dependence, we could say, with a little free thinking, that a co-dependent person gives selflessly, has awareness of other's needs, is committed to the outcome and is willing to take responsibility so that others don't have to risk the effort. Co-dependent people are very loyal. Co-dependent behavior informs how we feel our value or self-acceptance when others need us. There is always something we gain along our life journey when we pick up these shadow patterns that look negative on the outside, but internally they provided a benefit or served us at the time. Later, there may be an awareness that the shadow pattern or behavior isn't serving who we are now, so we can choose to heal that pattern and pick up co-empowerment as the new productive pattern.

Light and dark mirrors will always coexist. We cannot have a perception to see the light side, or even the light within the dark, without the contrast of the dark side. This is part of our design as a human and why we have free will to make new choices. If there was no need to choose between light and dark, we would not need to access the gift of our free will. As it is, we make good choices and not so good choices, and these create the experiences from which we learn and grow. It would be very challenging to evolve as a person if we never made any mistakes or if we never stepped into a dark pattern, thought or belief. We would already be perfect, and where can we grow from there?

Co-dependent people aren't necessarily low-functioning individuals who can barely hold their life together. In contrast, the clients I support through subtle, and not so subtle, co-dependent behaviors are highly functioning, success-driven individuals. They look like they have it all together on the outside, but their inside story is where they take the hit from this unbalanced giving and caretaking. My theory relates to their internal broken heart, or lack of self-love and self-acceptance that leads to co-dependent behaviors of over-giving, enabling, and rescuing, with high levels of energy output that block receptivity and creativity. This translates into many forms of burnout, wipeout, overwhelm, and a lack of fulfillment and loss of passion for life, all falling under the umbrella of too much stress.

Co-dependence is like a dance — we need a partner we can do the "co" and "dependent" moves with. The dance partner roles are interchangeable. If we do one role, we do all: Persecutor-Rescuer/ Enabler-Victim. I created the most angst when I was in rescuer mode. We can never change others around us who may still be caught in the tentacles of co-dependency, but we can shift our own attitude and choose to stop dancing that dance with our partners and learn the new steps for co-empowerment. Once we are aware of our own co-dependency, we can start to take responsibility for our over-giving, enabling, rescuing, and micromanaging behavior patterns. The other person may wonder what happened, what changed in our relationship, but once we stop dancing their dance, the relationship will change into something different. The relationship may dissolve completely or they may follow your lead and take up the new steps.

> We are only responsible for the steps we take
> and the boundaries, agreements, or bottom
> lines we create. When we focus on our changed
> engagement, the relationship dynamics will
> change without having to change the other
> person.
> We *change us* to change the relationship. The
> other person may change or not, but it is not up
> to us to make that happen.

The true healing of co-dependence is when we learn to give to ourselves as fully as we give to others. When we learn to take a step back from rescuing and enabling another, we are allowing the other person to learn from their experience. We stop stealing their growth opportunity when we take a step back to support without stepping in to take over, staying in our own lane and allowing them to be inside theirs.

> Even though we have a caring intent, our efforts
> will disempower others if we do it for them.

Every time we jump in to rescue someone from a challenging situation they can learn from or enable someone to continue a sabotaging pattern they are stuck in, we are prolonging their pain and suffering by blocking their capacity to explore autonomy and learn from both their own mistakes and their illuminations.

> The conversation changes from, "Let me help you," to, "That sounds really tough. What are your options to meet this challenge?"

The art of co-empowerment is to deeply listen, to support the other person in their discomfort and to stay in our own circle using bottom lines and boundaries. This involves clearly discerning what is ours to do and what is theirs to do or from which to grow. This is a choice point of how we support another to truly take responsibility for their own choices, actions and outcomes.

Supporting them to work towards their own solution will empower them and increase their measure of self-worth. Co-empowerment is non-judgmental and supports the autonomy or self-governance of another to grow from their own insights and experiences, as well as learning how to take responsibility for the outcomes and consequences of their choices and priorities.

Letting go of our attachment to helping others takes real discernment to recognize in the situation when it is most supportive to release them into their own free will choice. It's about allowing another to live in the fullest experience, raw and real, so they gain a valuable life lesson for their own growth as we listen, support and challenge the steps they can take from a place of self-responsibility. They learn to stretch their own wings to meet the challenge. Some would call this tough love, and it will take discipline to stand back and not be the fixer, rescuer or enabler. Choosing to stand back to allow another to be in the fullness of their life situation is not easy and it may feel stressful at first, in fact, it may feel like torture! Letting go of control and reining in the desire to step in is where the healing comes for both parties.

Practice: Co-empowered Communication through Listening-Supporting-Challenging

One of the key steps when responding to stress triggers is to stay out of reactivity in our communication. It's important to take responsibility for our actions and our words, rather than going into blame, judgment or defensiveness. It can be automatic to go into blame and not take responsibility for what is ours to do or for which we are accountable. We don't want to enable and rescue others from what is within their scope to do. The expression "stay in your own lane" is the key for boundaries and developing co-empowered relationships. Discerning what is mine and what is yours is essential to not taking on other people's stuff and for taking responsibility for what is your stuff.

> The key component of co-empowered communication is to not control or micromanage the experiences of others, to not try to fix or problem solve other people's challenges or to offer advice.

We can allow the other person to take responsibility for what is theirs to do, and to learn from their mistakes and gain their own insights and refinement opportunities from their actions. We do this when we listen and simply hold space for the other person as they speak. On the other hand, internally we may feel reactive, resistant or want to project blame onto others. What will help us to simply notice our internal response and to hold back from our rescuer tendencies that want to jump in to fix or problem solve for them. You can't listen to support someone if you are busy reacting to what they are saying!

Listener-Supporter-Challenger Technique for Mindful Listening
When talking with our kids, partner, parents or co-workers, we can shift out of our reactivity and fix-it mentality when we approach our communication with a listening mode of staying focused on what the other person is saying. This takes practice, as we are breaking the old habit of formulating our response to another while they are communicating with us.

> Learning how to listen, support and challenge in
> our communication with another will conserve
> our energy while empowering the other person
> to take responsibility for their own process.

We don't need to fix their problems, offer advice, or share what happened to us as we simply hold space for another and listen, without thinking of our response or reacting in some way other than holding an attitude of non-judgment and neutrality in our demeanor.

Listen: When we listen to another and really hear them, they feel heard and met. Our deepest listening is not only from the physical ears on our head, but also from our heart and our womb or one-point, down in that power place in the belly. To be centered and listening from our core is being open-hearted in our mode of communication. This helps us to stay mentally and emotionally neutral and be present without distraction while we listen.

When we focus on only listening, we are not thinking or cultivating a response, we are not preparing a nugget of advice, or preparing a solution to offer. We are simply practicing the skill of listening fully to what the other person is saying. We are breathing and pausing, even in the simplest of communication exchange. There is no multitasking on any level.

Support: By listening, we can then support the other person as we stay neutral to hear their point of view. We are holding space with an attitude of non-judgement, even if we don't agree with them. We are supporting them with an "I have your back" non-verbal energetic that will clearly meet them where they are.

Challenge: Then we can challenge them. Here is where it's important to self-manage our desire to fix and problem solve. Here is where we empower them to have their own experience and learning opportunity. We offer a reflection that puts the action back onto the other person. A reflection is a statement of the truth you are witnessing and supports the person to take ownership of their situation. You can offer a few words back that are a simple statement of the facts as a neutral statement that is 100% focused on them. You may even parrot their own words as they describe their reality. We may say, "I hear you are in a tight spot. What is your plan to meet this deadline?" Or "What are your options to get through this?" Or "What are you learning from this?" To parrot their words, you may repeat back their words "you are overwhelmed and don't know where to start" or "You are frustrated."

Practicing this listener-supporter-challenger mode of communication is not coming from a place that we don't care. It is communicating that, "I trust that you have the courage to figure this out. I have your back if you need my support, and I have faith that you will find your way through this in your own timing."

Listening in this mode is communicating empathy, not sympathy, as sympathy can elicit pity and disempowerment. Empathy is what will empower another to meet adversity and personally grow from what they learn from the engagement. Holding space to be with another experiencing adversity instead of jumping in to rescue them from their tension, will provide more opportunity for their growth and increase their measure of self-worth.

CHAPTER 7: HOW OVER-GIVING LEADS TO SELF-FORGETTING (AND BURNOUT)

"Never give from the depths of your well, but from your overflow."

RUMI

The "Do-Gooder" syndrome, as I call it, is a pattern where we become so focused on doing for others that we forget to pencil ourselves into our own life. We tend to be over-giving if we are consistently prioritizing the needs of others first and putting ourselves on the bottom of our own to-do list. Some individuals are naturally very generous and giving of their time and energy, and others may have work values of being thorough and timely in the quality of their efforts, which gives them the reputation of being dependable and competent. If any of these qualities or characteristics apply to you, as they did for me, you may be the constant target as the go-to for everyone else's projects, which risk-taking priority over your personal plans. You may identify with the term "people-pleaser."

I felt overly responsible — for myself, for others, for everything around me. I believed it was up to me to see something through because others simply could not, or would not, follow through. I told myself, "I'm the one with the skills to do this job." This led to my over-commitment and inability to say no. Believing it was my responsibility to get the job done as others were counting on me, I couldn't possibly let them down without feeling guilty. One of my values is to follow through on commitments I have said yes to — and that's the attitude that created my patterns of rescuing, enabling and over-giving that felt disempowering. Every time I said yes to someone, I would forget my promise to myself and ignore my heart's desire as I consistently put the priorities and needs of others first.

Whether we are constantly saying yes to the requests of others, or we feel responsible to take charge for others by volunteering, we may have a tendency to over-commit ourselves and have a hard time saying no. The result is that our giving can become resentful or overwhelming. We may even try to say no, but without a clear internal no, or bottom line, we keep a back door open, turning our no into a maybe. This sounds something like, "No, I can't help you, but if you are really desperate let me know and I will see what I can do."

As I've already mentioned, my attempts to say no typically left a back door that could be accessed by a determined person. I lacked bottom lines and boundaries. It was excruciating to say no without a litany of reasons, which also contributed to the back door being left open for a maybe.

I *finally* learned that having personal
agreements *with myself* in the form of bottom
lines and boundaries is how I respect my time
and energy resources.

In this over-giving pattern, we naturally default to keeping our personal needs, wants and desires at the bottom of our priorities, often meaning there is no time for ourselves after we take care of our commitments to family, friends, community and work. It's a long list that keeps us running from thing to thing, like a hamster in a wheel. Instead of joyfully giving, we may feel frustrated, burdened, depleted, judgmental, bitter, angry or spread too thin with our time and energy. Our inner voice may sound like, "Why is it always up to me to get it done?"

Over-giving will take a toll on our happiness, health and fulfillment when we don't prioritize our "me" time to do those things that fill our energy tank. Over time, we lose connection to even knowing what we really want in terms of our personal heart's desire. It may feel like our inner desire disappeared or numbed out, so we just can't tune into what we want in terms of our desires. It's like a muscle we are not using that gets flabby when we ignore our needs, will and desires.

Over time, it becomes so much easier to fulfill the desires of others than figure out our own desires. Many times, we become both complacent and compliant to the will of others, which feels very disempowering. When there is a decision to be made, we will defer to the other person because we don't even know how to tune in to what we desire. It feels like the path of least resistance if we go along with what the other person wants and not be the decision maker. Alternatively, we are the peacekeepers and do not want to make waves. When we do decide, we feel doubt that we made the "right" choice in terms of *what the other person wants*, therefore, still not stepping fully into our own choice. This is a convoluted way to make decisions and prioritize, by thinking in fast thought so we can stay one step ahead to guess what the other person would choose.

It's tricky to jump through the mental hoops of our inner dialogue and still sound like we have a timely answer to offer. The inner dialogue may sound like this, "I will make a decision where to go to dinner after I figure out what your decision is. That way I can make the right choice that would suit you." I'm describing how my internal reality was for years to give you an example of how far I went to feel love, acceptance, and security from another. By making decisions this way, I did not take any responsibility for my personal heart's desires and choices. I was unable to speak up for myself or tune in to my heart's desire.

This pattern sets us up to look outside ourselves for validation and approval, not trusting our own inner guidance. We worry about what others will think of us and we fear disapproval and judgment, which makes us feel unloved or not accepted. To avoid disapproval or not meeting the expectations of others, we compensate by trying for perfection to avoid mistakes. We constantly feel worried about disappointing others, but it's our own inner judgment of our self that is disempowering our own self-authority, not the other person.

> At the heart of over-giving and being overly
> focused on others is our need to feel love,
> acceptance and security on the *inside* through
> *outside* validation.

Most learned from a very early age the pain of punishment and isolation. We learned that being a "good girl" or "good boy" was rewarded with approval and a sense of feeling loved and rewarded by the key individuals who influenced us in our life. Our image makers influenced our behavior in many ways, both positive and negative, like a lump of clay that is formed into a desired shape.

If our individual expression was repressed by the significant people in our life, like mine was, then the pattern of being approval-driven becomes encoded as a deeply rooted behavior. Repression, or hiding, of our individual expression or choice can occur whenever we perceive that our words or actions are repeatedly rejected by others, specifically, the times that expressing our individuality or speaking up for ourselves went against the flow of our image makers and was not accepted or rewarded.

Going against the norms or expectations of others may have resulted in being punished, ridiculed, bullied, or some response that was perceived as rejection, and shut down our individuality. We did not feel safe or a sense of belonging, and therefore lacked self-acceptance until we came back into alignment with what others wanted or expected from us in terms of our behavior, attitude and verbal expressions.

Ultimately, we learned to reject our individuality, and to feel insecure in our self-expression, learning to compensate by excelling in approval-seeking behaviors. Fast forward to our adult years, and we can see how the patterns of co-dependency leading to over-giving were created.

Being a good (fill in the blank: parent/child/spouse/employee) by being "other focused" as a people-pleaser is slavery when we are at the beck and call to serve. We over commit. Our selfless giving can become overwhelming when we are always the one who is called for action or follow through, and the joy of giving becomes a burden and feels like a "should do" and not a "want to." Burnout is a reality when we do not have the bandwidth for recharge activities to fill our energy tank.

Freedom is experienced when we exercise our free will muscle and step into our autonomy, or self-governance, by reclaiming our space and saying YES! to our heart's desire as our priority. This is not indulgence, but an act of self-care. Saying yes to ourself and doing for ourself is how we add fuel to our inner fire to feel passion and joy. But for some of us, saying yes to ourselves may trigger inner stress and guilt when we are not doing what we "should" for others. What can support us to do more things for ourselves is when we identify which of our personal values we are supporting when we give to our SELF. Here are examples of how to identify the value you are feeding when you prioritize your desires. Note that what makes the activity a core value for one person will be different for another:

- What is it about shopping for a sale that you value? Is it stalking the bargain or expressing your individuality through your wardrobe? You may not have shopping in any form as a value, but it could be something about creating financial stability in your life if shopping for essentials.
- What do you love about a weekend away? Is it the value of seeing a new landscape or being spontaneous when you are out of your routine?

- What value are you supporting when you engage in your hobby? Golf or fishing may support your connection to nature. Painting, crafting, or gardening may be your door into mindfulness. These activities still the mind when you are in the zone of timelessness and total presence with focus, doing the activity you love to do. Hobbies can become a practice for mindful awareness.
- Getting lost in a good book may support your value for imagination and creativity or tapping into the unknown with a mystery.

This is true self-care, when we can recognize *why* the activity or thing we do to fill our tank is important to us. When something has personal value or importance, it will feel like a desire or a "want to," and not a commitment like a "should do." Learning to say yes to self and no to others without feeling guilty is the true gift of healing we give to ourselves, with self-respect and honor for our personal needs and desires. Turning this pattern around is a practice of self-devotion to train a new pattern of saying yes to our heart's desire. Picking up tools, tips and practices is how to take steps to re-wire the pattern of over-giving that leads to the stress-induced self-forgetting.

We are true to ourselves when we keep our agreements with ourselves, which may mean saying no to another. Taking a stand for what we need and desire requires both self-authority and self-worth to speak up so we can take responsibility for our own happiness. It takes courage to turn this pattern around, as well as a new perspective on how to do self-care. When we are true to our personal values and priorities, we can say yes to ourselves with an attitude of "to thine own self be true" as our new mantra for setting priorities. This simple concept is not so easy to carry forward. If it was, we would already be doing it. To truly honor ourselves, we need bottom lines and boundaries, without a back door that is like a wobbly loophole for someone to still get a yes from us when we really want to be a no.

It takes focus and strategy to be able to speak the unspeakable at times and stand up for ourselves. Learning how to be true to self takes courage. It takes practice to re-wire the new pattern as it feels so foreign and risky initially, but the rewards of speaking truthfully and expressing honestly are incredibly empowering. Every time we speak up for ourselves, we make a direct deposit into our self-worth bank account. When we feel heard and met in our communication with others, we can hold our ground and stay calm in a discussion.

Tuning up my communication skills was something concrete I worked on to improve. A big part of stress mastery boils down to a shift in how we are communicating to transform both internal communication with self and external communication with others. Once we learn the secret of how to do this, we will make a positive impact on all our relationships.

Preventing burnout by fueling your tank takes being a good steward of your energy resources.

Every time we give our energy to our work, family and community, we are spending energy from our inner resources. If we give and give to others as a people-pleaser, we will get to a point where we deplete our energy because we are not balanced in how we are keeping our own energy tank full. Remember the expression to "put on your own oxygen mask first?" Energy resources are parallel to our financial resources. If every time we gave our energy to help others, we also gave them some of our cash or wrote them a check, we would eventually go bankrupt if we didn't add money deposits to our checking account, which equates to our day-to-day spending. If we do deplete our checking account, we may go to our savings account. This is a problem, because our savings account equates to our life force energy, our chi/ki, or creative Soul force energy.

If we tap into our Soul force resources and deplete our inner resources, we will feel burned out. Our inner fire and passion for life goes out, our creativity is gone, and we lose access to our motivation. We lose our mojo! We are at risk of opening the door to a serious physical illness or emotional mood disturbance. And no surprise, our sense of well-being feels flat. We can lose hope as we disconnect from what brings us meaning and purpose.

The most stress-resilient people are those who regularly do the little things that keep their energy tank full. Prioritizing activities that bring joy, fun and pleasure is like adding fuel to the fire for passion and joy in life. It's the simple things, like coffee with a friend, playing card games with your family, hiking in nature, and engaging in creative projects. Practicing spontaneity to say yes to a heart's desire activity in the moment is another way to strengthen your free will muscle and fuel up with pleasure.

The interesting thing about these pleasure-filled moments is that many are linked to mindful awareness. Any activity that pulls us into a quiet focus, stops time and shuts the distractions out is a channel to tap into mindfulness practice. When we can access "the zone" doing the activities we love, our inner dialogue is quiet as we access a Zen moment and fill our energy bank at the same time. This quiet, focused state of mindful awareness can be cross trained to create more inner resources to access stress resilience when we need to respond to life's happenings.

Folding these activities that we truly hunger for regularly into our lifestyle diet is the ultimate self-care. When we keep our tank full with "me time" we have more to give to others and there is no scarcity of our precious energy resources, so our giving is joyful and heartfelt. In shamanism we learn to honor self, life and others in that order — not others, life and self.

Practice: Feeding Your Hungers Technique
Make a list of at least five or six activities you love to do that are relaxing, fun, restorative and pleasurable. These are not the big bucket list things, but the simple pleasures you enjoy in your day — the same activities that often get pushed off the radar when you're busy. You may tell yourself that you'd like to do these things someday when you have more time. The target here is to prioritize what you want to do in terms of what will support your recharge.

There is no time too short for what brings in more pleasure and relaxation to restore your energy when they are worthy hungers to feed. They may also have an added health benefit to calm your nervous system from the fight-or-flight stress response.

The important perspective here is that you are looking for the things that you *want* to do, not prioritizing the things you *should* do, like a checklist of to-dos. If they do feel like a should, or don't provide an energy boost, explore a way that it feels lighter, like a "want-to" in terms of feeling like a heart's desire. Adding something to bring in more pleasure or fun, such as listening to music or an audio book during your engagement with an activity, may increase your motivation.

Guilt is often an emotional trigger when you get caught in the *should do* versus the *want to*. For example, we may say, "I want to sit on the patio and read this book," but think, "I should be doing something with my family." Doing for ourselves is how we receive energy input. We may need to accommodate both values for ourselves and our family with a "yes and" approach, where we allow ourselves some reading time and we spend some time with our family.

> **When we honor our values, we will increase our internal motivation to follow through. When we model self-care to others, we set the tone for them to do the same for themselves, giving permission for "me time." Making sure we have "me time" is essential for restoring ourselves so we can show up more fully for others and potentially deepen our connection.**

Fulfilling our heart's desire daily is how we can cross-train receptivity. How we give our own gifts to ourselves, rather than always sharing our gifts with others, is a form of self-healing.

Practice: 30-Day Feeding Your Heart's Desire

One simple practice is to do at least one thing per day that is pure heart's desire. Track this practice daily, until you can sustain thirty consecutive days of fulfilling at least one thing that is your heart's desire per day.

If you miss a day, start over at day one and track your daily practice until you can sustain a consecutive thirty-day practice.

This practice is quite challenging if you are someone who does a lot for others. It supports you to exercise your spontaneity muscle, while training you to curb the outflow of your energy and to focus on how to be receptive to your own giving of your energy to yourself. Tuning into what you desire and taking action to give it to yourself is very nourishing for your heart and fuels your happiness.

CHAPTER 8: COURAGEOUS RELATIONSHIPS

"Some people come in our life as blessings.
Some come in your life as lessons."

Mother Teresa

As someone living an adventurous life fueled by edgy learning experiences and exploring deep ceremonial spaces, I'm not sure if I'm a courageous woman or a crazy woman. I can put myself out in front even when I'm about to keel over from anxiety and nervousness. I have learned to be skillful at many practices and strategies to maintain my cool externally in the face of almost debilitating performance anxiety.

I feel the instant the stress hormones of fight-or-flight kick in to rev up my system into overdrive, and learned to rely on their juice to push me forward into the eye of the storm. I seem to be the one who says yes to every opportunity that comes my way, whether it's realistic to add to my plate or not. I've learned to love public speaking, despite nerves that make me shake. I push through performance anxiety when I'm being observed and being offered feedback from my teachers to meet the "standards of excellence" of alchemy during my training. I remember feeling the juice of my stress hormones while standing in the center of a suspension bridge over a raging river while trekking in the Himalayas, and feeling my heart pound as I stood at the top of a black diamond ski run before I pushed off for my first turn.

> In my past, the thrill of the stress hormone rush
> was what supported me to take the next step
> beyond my comfort zone so I could forge ahead.
> I've learned to do it differently now, after many
> years of feeling addicted to stress hormones to
> give me the push into action.

During high school, I was a cheerleader and felt zero insecurity or nervousness about standing in front of the crowd, shouting cheers and jumping around with the athletic antics of the cheers we created. The funny part is that I was an enthusiastic cheerleader, but I know nearly zero about the rules of football or basketball. I just loved leading the crowd into a whipped-up frenzy of emotionally charged cheering and excitement.

Standing in front of the grandstands was easy, being in front of a group is fun even now as a teacher, speaker, and in my other leadership roles. But put me in front of one person, that's where I am at my true edge. Engaging in one-on-one relationships is when I'm swimming in my insecurity and lack of emotional safety.

I've been able to bluff my way through most one-on-one relationships, except for relationships with men and authority figures. I feel deep-rooted fear when presented with commitment to intimate relationships. It has taken the sum of my experiences over my life to unveil and see the truth about this arena of life for me. It has been my blind spot. My life has had many blessings and rich opportunities, but the one area of longing for more confidence would have to be in my relationship arena.

I can look back and see my pattern with connection avoidance was there from the time I was a teenager, and probably earlier, but it was only recently that I could name what I was feeling in those one-on-one relationships. The word popped in so loudly from my intuition that I nearly jumped out of my skin. The word was "unsafe" and the phrase was "I don't feel safe." Once that word was out, I immediately saw my life pass in front of my eyes — all the young men and grown men who have approached me for a date, a relationship, or even a conversation. These males are either safe or not safe. Those who are safe are in rock-solid committed relationships, or perhaps older and energetically patriarchal. The not safe are those who are not in relationships. Men who are interested, attracted, and available put me on edge. I rejected many men along the way. Even those who joined me in relationship did not stay emotionally connected with me because of the unconscious barrier I had around maintaining my safety.

The pattern is, "Let's just be friends. I really like you, so why would we ruin a perfectly good friendship by having a relationship?" Or if I did enter a relationship, there was the rubber band movement back and forth of moving in close emotionally, but then moving back out again. Feeling close and then pulling away, like "push-me-pull-you" energy. This rubber band energetic was a repeating theme for me because I am attracted to men who are just as emotionally unavailable as I am. Ironically, they are "safe" when they are emotionally unavailable, therefore I am more likely to allow them into my life.

I recognized what was happening to sabotage my relationships, but didn't understand why it was so difficult to feel a strong, empowering connection with another. I would alternately give away my power from co-dependency (feeling insecure when I wanted to feel loved, liked and included) or push them away with my self-reliance. The other quality of my relationships is that once they end, the relationship feels stronger and therefore better, as I can relax, let down my guard and my expectations and feel safe again. Yet in my heart of hearts, I want to commit and find a deeply fulfilling and lasting relationship. I have not yet been able to create this for myself, despite being partnered with some very gifted and amazing men.

This concept of not feeling safe with another was a significant epiphany. Of course, I had to look at the male image makers from my past to unpack this one. I didn't think I would write about my father in this book, but here it is, not with blame or resentment, but to recognize how I took in his parenting style as the first "man" in my life. It is with deep respect and love for him that I share our story.

My father was a prolific and visionary entrepreneur who had many irons in the fire of his multiple business projects. He was a creative Soul with a free spirit. He worked a lot, and in those days, there were no mobile phones, no text messages, and the technology we now enjoy in our daily lives had not yet been invented. When he left the house, he was gone for long periods. When he was home, he was often working outside in the yard, or napping on the couch. When we sat around the dinner table he was there, but not really present, in the sense that he was very quiet. Some evenings he worked through dinner and wasn't home.

As I look back, I see my dad as a generous and excellent provider for our family. I now recognize that he was not emotionally available as the protector of the family, primarily related to his absence from home to work and his lack of presence with the family when he was home. I have two older brothers who tormented me to tears every day. They were rarely checked by my parents, who simply thought their behavior typical as "boys will be boys." Sibling teasing may be a normal phenomenon within sibling rivalry, but it had a profound impact on my self-worth. I remember feeling that I would do anything to be included by my brothers and to feel liked and accepted by them. Whatever I did to gain their attention just egged them on for more antics of torment, much of which made great stories, but drove me to tears at the time.

My father did things with my brothers in which I was never included. My little girl perception was that there were rules for the boys and a different set of rules for the girl. I was raised under the stern eye of my mother. She was in charge of me, just as my father was in charge of the boys. Two standards for parenting. I always felt loved by my father, but he just wasn't around for me in my early years. My perception was that my brothers had more freedom than I did and that they would prefer that I didn't hang around them. If I tried to engage with them they would say things like, "Thank you, Miss Information," (aka misinformation). They loved to tell me jokes to see if I would laugh. Sometimes their jokes were not meant to be funny, on purpose, to see if I would laugh anyway. This sent them into hysterics when I fell for their tricks, which felt very demoralizing to me. My brothers had a lot of laughs at my expense.

One of my father's weaknesses was his pattern with alcohol. When we were young kids, we would say that Dad was "ho-ho-ho-ish," as he became jolly when he had a few drinks. I later described my dad as a man who loved "wine, women and song" in that he was someone who knew how to have a good time and he thrived in spontaneity.

In my teen years and beyond, my father drank on a daily basis and his intoxication triggered shame and pity within me, as if I was responsible for his condition in some way. I wanted to cover for him so others would not see he had a problem with alcohol. This behavior added to my burden of feeling responsible, as if I were the worried parent, and contributed to my patterns of self-reliance and emotional distance. I experienced shame, especially when he was intoxicated in public. I didn't understand his pain during those years, but can see his insecurity and fear more clearly now. This was the point when I started burying myself in schoolwork, setting me up for my career working patterns. The fruit doesn't fall far from the tree. Stay busy so I am not emotionally available, work harder to numb my feelings of inadequacy, and don't allow anyone in too close.

As a teenager, the atmosphere at home changed when my dad and I started doing father-daughter things together, like long bike rides and trips to go snow skiing. I became a Daddy's girl as we spent more time together. My brothers treated me nicer too once they left home. When I spent time with my dad, one-on-one, he was often distracted. He did not often meet my gaze when talking with me, but gazed around the room or watched other people. This was how we communicated when we were together.

My dad was generous in his giving of material needs and gifts, but what I missed was the feeling of security and trust that he would follow through on his word. He was noncommittal. I never knew if he would remember his promises, so I learned to not have expectations for follow through or to feel disappointed if plans changed. Instead, I had expectations that the plans would likely change. I learned to believe that in the eyes of others, my needs and desires were not important. I learned to become self-reliant and independent to not count on the promises of others, and to take care of myself.

I had a core belief that I was responsible, and everything was up to me. I adopted a philosophy in my engagements of "I won't share what I really want, because your needs are more important than mine." This led to separation and emotional distance rather than building the intimacy, connection, and shared vision that creates cohesion within relationships. What I gained from this belief was to be the manifester of my own dreams and aspirations, without the support of others.

My parents didn't share common interests in terms of leisure and lifestyle activities. Dad was a goer and Mother was a homebody. A big challenge for them was that Dad, in his noncommitment, would often say, "Let's play it by ear," which drove my mother crazy, because she was a planner and wanted to nail down the details. I felt the fallout from their lack of marital cohesion. They stayed married but lived very separate lives, and I often felt like the connecting link between them. This solidified my resolve unconsciously to always be in a position where I could take care of myself independently of anyone else and be my own supporter and provider.

The tension I felt with my parents created the undertone of not feeling safe in my personal relationships, which created an unconscious emotional barrier to really bond myself to another. This was the flavor of my "emotionally unavailable," burying myself in studies or work and not having time or attention to give to another person. I still remember the time my dad came to visit me at college when I had a lot of homework as finals were approaching. He came on the spur of the moment, and I remember feeling guilty because I knew I needed to study and I was torn about spending time with him after he'd made the effort to come for a visit. I didn't know how to negotiate a win-win agreement to prioritize my studies and enjoy my visit with him, so I ended up feeling really horrible and ashamed in my conflict of study time versus Dad time.

I can look back and see the pattern of how often I made work (or homework) my priority over people. I appeared to be career driven, but my motivation was to feel safe, to feel in control and create my own inner security and self-reliance. I didn't have enough self-awareness to be able to share these insights with others and negotiate what I needed to feel safe and secure in the presence of another.

People assume that because I'm career focused and successful that I'm a woman who chose to not marry or have children. Truth is, I repressed the longing I felt to share life experiences with someone I could call my partner with my business. Instead, I filled my life with working, being of service, and loaded my calendar up with a lot of doing to fill my inner space. I've created a life filled with experiences that would likely not have happened if I was focused on raising a family and living a more traditional lifestyle. I certainly would not be so deeply engaged in my spiritual pursuits as an apprentice of an ancient shamanic lineage. I feel more surprised than anyone about the trajectory my life took once I found my Spiritual Path. The door opened and I said yes.

This awareness of my engagements with men also translates to my sense of safety in all one-on-one relationships. I now categorize each personal engagement as safe, not safe, or starting to feel safe. I can tune into what I'm feeling in my body. When I don't feel safe, I can feel the tension in my solar plexus, almost becoming rock-hard energetically. I can now sense the relationships where I truly feel trust and safety and can relax and let down my guard energetically. I recognize the relationships where I'm not safe and can feel a perceptible internal energetic shake of tension. This discernment has been illuminating in my interactions with others.

Now that I'm aware, I will take the time I need to build trust and use open-hearted communication to move towards feeling safe with another. If I recognize that I'm feeling the internal shake, I can now name it as feeling vulnerable, which gives me the grace to simply be present with my inner truth. It has been an important step for me to take responsibility for what I need personally to feel safe in relationships and to clean up my part with those I have pushed away.

When I felt insecure, before my epiphany, I sabotaged my engagements in relationships with distraction, causing inattention, over-giving through over-doing, and deflection by not being receptive. Through self-awareness, I now identify my feelings of insecurity as vulnerability, which helps me to stay open to the conversation, even in my discomfort, and to be present and receptive. I imagine that my heart is open and I focus on my listening skills. I also recognize an important step for my self-care is to create my *inner sanctuary,* a safe space for me to stand inside my nervousness and vulnerability. I do this with the practice of coming "home" into my womb. Taking a deep breath, I anchor my energy to that place 2-3 finger breadths below my naval and a bit back towards my spine, into my one-point, and anchor my feet to connect into the earth. This practice is how I feel stable to stay present and connected with another.

I've been intentional about how I can make amends to the brotherhood who I may have wounded from my own emotional behavior patterns. I brought my desire for forgiveness into ceremony. I can stand in front of a crowd and lead a cheer or give a talk, but it's my one-on-one relationships where I shook. Nothing could change until I had the awareness of not feeling safe.

Once I saw the pattern, I could name the
pattern, and then I could change the pattern
when my intention was clear. Keeping my heart
open in my communication is my new pattern
of honesty that I dedicate myself to, and I can
only do that if I create my own inner sanctuary
first.

Practice: Creating Your Inner Sanctuary

To create inner security, it's important to intentionally assemble your inner sanctuary first so you can feel more stable and secure externally. The key in this practice is to create a way to come *home* into your body. The Light Globe Practice comes from Rachael Jayne Groover, the creator of the Art of Feminine Presence ®.

1. Consciously connect your feet to the earth to create a stable base.

2. Take three deep breaths into your one-point or womb/ dantian space, into the place 2-3 fingers below your naval and back towards your spine. Your center of gravity is here and will anchor your presence into the here and now. Deep breaths connect you with the rest-and-digest mode of stress resilience to trigger the parasympathetic nervous system to put the brakes on your stress response.

3. Light Globe Technique: Imagine your aura surrounds you, 360 degrees in all directions, as far as your arms can reach. Imagine your aura is a shield of protection and safety, in a light bulb shape, as a container for your energy. Your

feet are like the two filaments that connect you to the earth. This light globe will keep other people's energy from coming into your space and conserve your energy from leaking or spilling out. You can imagine the glass wall is as thick or as thin as you need to feel safe.

Steps 1 and 2 can be done routinely throughout your day to feel present and centered while engaging with others. You can assemble yourself inside your light globe (Step 3) any time you enter a space where others are present as an extra step for emotional safety and to conserve your precious lifeforce energy so you can be more magnetic.

CHAPTER 9: TURNING AROUND YOUR GUILT, BLAME, SHAME, DOUBT, AND FEAR

"Awakening is not changing who you are but discarding who you are not."

Deepak Chopra

Feeling stressed will push us into our default negative thinking and behavior patterns when we are triggered emotionally and mentally. This can show up as inner dialogue and negative emotions that will open the door to our sabotaging behavior patterns. Losing our emotional balance is at the heart of stress. Stress will trigger these blocks to our happiness and harmony and throw us into well-worn patterns that keep us stuck in our comfort zone, rather than expanding and growing at the edge of what is triggering our stress.

We each have a proclivity to one or more of these default patterns. Recognizing how we are engaging these blocks is the first step to turning them around so we can fully and authentically express ourselves. These blocks include all forms of guilt, shame, blame, doubt, insecurity, resistance, repression, and the biggie — fear.

Me — in a heartbeat I go straight into blame. How quickly my thoughts go outward to lay the responsibility on someone else. Let's say I can't find something in my kitchen. I live alone, but will go straight into blame thinking of "who did it," blaming my cleaning person or my latest houseguest with the assumption that they put it somewhere and now I can't find it. This is such a common reaction that it is comical for me. I laugh at myself, take a pause and retrace my last steps to locate the missing item.

Perhaps this one is more familiar to you, another favorite that I go to – doubt. When I'm in doubt about something, I'll tell myself I'm in confusion or that I lack clarity, ignoring that doubt is where I'm really stuck. Fear often accompanies doubt. When facing unfamiliar territory, I'll dive into my imagination, projecting dire outcomes in the future. Fear will also trigger my anxiety mode, where my mind can create wild scenarios based completely in fantasy, not reality. Shame within my belief system is a key area of self-healing for me in terms of my concepts of self as being worthy, good enough, smart enough, and self-deserving.

These blocks will sound familiar to us as we recognize how we get stuck when we allow them into our life. Once we are aware that we are doing one or more of these blocks, we can use the ally as a remedy to turn it around and rewire that pattern into a more empowering attitude and approach.

Read each of these blocks to see which ones ring true for you and how you can turn them around to stop the negative impact.

Guilt: We feel guilty if we perceive that we have done something wrong. To turn guilt around, ask yourself "What is the truth?" If you have done something wrong to another, then take responsibility and make amends. If you are confident you have not done anything wrong, then you will gain truth and step out of feeling guilty.

Others may try to manipulate you into guilt, or you may induce this state yourself if you focus on the "shoulds" in terms of what you should do versus what you want to do.

> A simple reality check can support an assessment
> of the TRUTH which will set you free.

When you are in conflict with your personal values and choose one over the other, you may feel guilty. Here is where a moment of truth, or a personal honesty assessment, can check if your values are in direct conflict with each other. This will set you free when you can clearly discern the choice you are making is values based (either your values or someone else's).

Shame: Experienced when we have a belief or see ourselves as a bad person, or feel there is something innately "wrong" with us.

> You feel shame when your measure of self-worth
> is low and if your poor self-concepts and pain
> or victim stories are encoded into your belief
> system as reality.

The turnaround or ally for shame happens when you have PRIDE or POISE in accepting what you have done well or what makes you a worthy person. Poise means to give yourself grace, balance or equilibrium. Rewiring shame from your belief system happens through reframing your value through the lens of reality, and self-recognition in the form of pride about your gifts, your shining or what you have done well in terms of your efforts or lessons learned.

Blame: A common habit when we blame self, life, and others and do not take responsibility for our actions.

The turnaround for blame is proper discernment to see what part is for you to take responsibility for. ACCEPTANCE is the gain when you take responsibility for what is yours to do, and the discernment of what belongs to someone else. You can see a lot of blame in our collective right now as prime examples.

> We can each do our part when we accept what is
> ours to take responsibility for so we can be part
> of the solution.

For example, if you lose your car keys, do you go to the blame of "who moved my keys?" or do you go into self-reflection of "where was I last when I had my keys?" Self-responsibility will support accurate discernment.

Doubt: Doubt will keep us stuck in inertia from analysis paralysis and not taking action.

> You may be making excuses or alibis and not
> taking responsibility for forward movement
> when you are in doubt. Doubt will keep you
> stuck in your safety net or comfort zone and
> not stretching into something new. Sometimes
> doubt looks like confusion.

Taking one step as a DECISIVE ACTION will get you out of inertia and doubt. You can always course correct if the step proves to not be the best action. Decisive action beats no action and moves you towards mastery. You will gain confidence when you turnaround your doubt by taking an action, even as one small step, which can move you beyond your stuck place in your comfort zone.

Insecurity: Relates to our feelings of uncertainty or anxiety when we lack confidence in our own value or capability. We lack trust in ourselves.

Insecurity can become *inner security* when you become aware of feelings of being unsure of yourself. Naming your insecurity and owning it, rather than shrinking from it, will provide outer SECURITY when you are *authentic and vulnerable* in your insecurity. Trust yourself that you are enough in terms of your value.

Standing in your own circle of empowerment to self-govern through your personal bottom lines and boundaries creates autonomy and builds self-respect. When you are true to yourself you create inner peace and gain outer confidence. Without bottom lines and boundaries, insecurity will open the door to co-dependence. This block is where you can invite the grace and humility to be honest with yourself, rather than trying to suppress or deflect your true feelings. A simple practice of pausing to notice the inner shake and taking a few deep breaths can help you through those insecure moments to stabilize inner peace.

Resistance: Blocks us from flow and may feel like we are living with the handbrake on, which costs a lot of precious life force energy.

> The longer you are in resistance, the more energy you will lose. It can look subtle, such as the ways you avoid engagement through distraction and procrastination, or it can look like kicking and screaming all the way until you finally take the leap out of resistance and jump headfirst into the fire.

When you take one step into action you will step out of resistance and into FLUIDITY and FLOW. Fluidity and flow are more energy conserving and can help you to get unstuck.

Resistance is a key factor behind much of our stress. Often what we are stressing about is linked to what we are resisting. We each do resistance in our own way. Some will wait and wait to take action until it's the eleventh hour or we're forced to make a move or the opportunity will pass us by. Some are surprised by the energy they are resisting and don't even see it coming until the situation is in their face. Others will fight the energy as their way to resist.

Our internal readiness to change, or to meet a challenge, may impact how we engage with our resistance. Making the decision to prioritize one baby step is all it takes to get into flow and out of feeling stuck in our resistance.

Moving through resistance can come in stages:

- In the precontemplation phase, we deny there is a problem to solve. We are blind to it and in full resistance to change because it is not even on our radar when we have no self-awareness of the need to take action.
- In the contemplation phase we are thinking about making a change, but have still not put an action into place. We may be sitting in ambivalence or considering the pros and cons of taking action. We may stew here for some time until we have our "why" as the priority or decision to engage with action.
- In the planning phase we are ready to think about taking action and formulating a way to break free from our resistance.
- In the action phase we are taking steps and are in the flow or fluidity of change and out of resistance. We may actually gain energy from the steps we take using our chi/ki to move through our resistance. Our attitude may shift from "I should" to "I can" or "I will."

Many times, when we feel stress, we are in a state of resistance about something. The longer we resist, the longer we will experience our stress patterns. The longer we are in stress, the more energy we lose.

On point with the theme that one of the key methods to gain more energy is to stop losing it, when we can stop procrastinating, distracting, stalling, or postponing, we can stop the energy leak.

Attention = Power is in effect here too. *Where our focus goes is what grows.* If we focus on our distraction, we will get more of that. If we focus on the decision we can make or one step we can take to engage with what we are resisting, we will unblock our energy flow and step out of resistance and into action.

The first step towards decisive action and taking that first baby step is *your awareness to simply notice and name your resistance without judgment or concern.* "Isn't that interesting how I'm reading email articles instead of writing my proposal." Or "Notice how I'm organizing my closet instead of making that phone call." You might even have a chuckle when you catch yourself in the act, and then you can make a choice to focus on your next step towards that thing about which you are resisting and stressing.

Repression: happens when we are hiding or holding back in our life in some way. It can look like you are invisible or feel like you are trying to stay under the radar.

You will not fully express your shining or your gifts when in repression, living inside a self-imposed box of limitations, or wearing a self-inflicted mask of conformity that hides your true nature.

Repression may look like not putting your hand up for opportunities to stretch or grow, choosing instead to stick with your comfort zone rather than risk failure, disappointment, judgment or criticism. You may be worried about the perception of others towards you.

You may not be aware of your box, or of being in a state of repression, until you are confronted to grow or change in some way. This "courage at the edge" approach to grow beyond repression will come as a direct deposit towards your measure of self-worth when you accept the confrontation and step out of your box to stretch beyond what is safe and familiar.

Using your imagination to see a new vision, beyond your stuck place, will help you see how you can expand beyond your box of the comfort zone that is holding you back from growing. Inspire yourself by stretching your IMAGINATION ("I the magi" as my teacher said) to see what is possible if you step out and take a risk to shine or grow in some way.

Stepping into a new or bigger space and putting yourself out in a new and authentic way takes imagination to dream yourself into it. You dream it first as a vision, then you bring your vision into your life as a reality when you take those first baby steps into the new direction.

Fear: A big one, fear is mostly related to fear of the unknown versus fear of physical harm.

What you don't know may terrify you and keep you stuck in your comfort zone, as the devil you know, and not taking the leap of faith into change. Taking steps to gain KNOWLEDGE about the unknown, or to make the unknown knowable, will turn your fear into courage.

The more you can learn about what you fear, the more courage you will gain. Knowledge will dissolve the unknown and reduce the scary factor, setting you free to dip your toe in the water to explore something new.

> Your greatest awakening may be lurking behind
> that blind spot you've been avoiding due to your
> fear.

Fear can show up in many forms if we let it rule our lives, and is often linked to our resistance. Fear can keep us stuck in a rut so we don't take the steps to break free from our safety net. Fear of mistakes or of failure may keep us stuck in inertia. Allowing our fear to hold us back from growth opportunities will keep us living small. We may tolerate those things that are unsatisfying to keep the peace and avoid disappointing another. We may choose to stay in an unfulfilling relationship because our fear of losing the relationship is greater than the desire to gain something new or different. Fear may make us complacent, even if our comfort zone is unsatisfying.

> It is primarily the unknown consequences of
> change that we fear the most.

Which of these blocks do you recognize in yourself? I know I have a couple of "go-to's" that I need to be aware of. Simply paying attention and noticing how we are engaging with any of these blocks is essential to turning them around so we are not stuck in our shadow thoughts, inner dialogue and sabotaging responses.

Self-awareness is the first step to see how we are obstructing our own happiness and harmony with these blocks that become habitual. Rewiring the turnaround will provide truth, acceptance, confidence, security, pride, fluidity, imagination, and courage to step out of the safety of the comfort zone and into forward expansion and transformation.

> Our first step to turn around any of these blocks
> is our self-awareness to catch the moment when
> we are doing them. Once we have the ah-ha, we
> can take the next step of the formula to find the
> turnaround.

These blocks cause a type of stress that is very internal and leads to being stuck in charged negative emotions that block us from moving through the emotions as "energy in motion." To put this into context, within my shamanic lineage, emotions relate to the element of water. Balanced emotions move like a flowing stream of water, while unbalanced emotions are either frozen like an iceberg, turbulent like rough waters, or stagnant like toxic waters.

> When your emotional energy is moving freely
> as "energy in motion," you can feel more
> energized, balanced and resilient to meet
> challenges. Emotional energy that is stuck
> and not moving, or is expressed as turbulent
> emotionality, is exhausting.

We open the door to health problems and experience a lack of happiness and harmony when we are not fluid with our emotions in terms of moving through them as "energy in motion." For example, if you typically push through your resentment or hunker down into it, you can throw off your health and wellbeing. When we get caught up in emotional drama or swirling around in the emotionality of resentment, we can experience a negative impact on our health and happiness over time.

Energy in motion is how we learn to experience our emotions from our heart space, whatever they are, within the full emotional spectrum of our human-beingness, and to let them go as a giving energy, rather than being stuck in them as a holding energy or swirling around in our emotions like a receiving energy. Picking up tools, tips and practices is one way to move through the negative emotions so we can restore our emotional balance and control, which ultimately increases our energy flow and supports our happiness.

Give-aways to Rebalance Our Emotions and Stop the Energy Leak
In my spiritual community we do something called a "give-away," where we give away our negative energy, thoughts and feelings to a tree. It's important to restore our emotional balance and harmony as a way to conserve our precious energy, maintain stable health and invest in our happiness. And it's important to name what the negative feeling is when we feel triggered by people or situations and events. If we ruminate about our negative thoughts and feelings, we may trigger the fight-or-flight stress response. The longer we stay stuck in our emotional soup, the more energy we will lose.

> To master our stress and access the meet-the-
> challenge mode of stress resilience, we need
> to release our negativity and rebalance our
> emotions to stop the emotional discharge that
> depletes our energy resources.

This is what is meant with the concept that healthy emotions are *energy in motion* which is more energy conserving than spinning our wheels inside swirling emotionality.

Practice: Give-away to a Tree

Find a tree that you feel drawn towards. Make a connection and ask it to work with you. It can be any tree near your home or office, or in a park if you are not close to nature. Your negative energy will not harm the tree. Trees connect you to nature at those times when you can't logistically put yourself into nature to restore your balance and harmony.

Here's how you do it:

- Find any tree that you feel drawn to work with and walk three times clockwise around the tree to connect energetically with the tree.
- Stand with your front facing the tree to connect with the tree, then talk to the tree to give away any negative feelings, frustrations, anger, sadness, rage, or fear.
- Say in the first person, present tense, "I give away…" (name what the negative energy is).
- Speak from your heart. Say it out loud, unless people are around.
- If you feel like you need to cut away from the negative energy, you can take your hand and sweep down from above your head, down your front and say, "I cut away from… (name the energy or the person)" in a voice of command.

- Thank the tree for supporting you when you're complete. You can give the tree a hug or some of your essence in the form of saliva or a strand of your hair.

The tree can take your negative feelings and give them away to the Universe, like stinky fertilizer or compost that promotes green growth. Trees are resilient. Their roots connect to the earth as they grow towards the light, reaching for the sky and connecting us to God or our Higher Power, and all that is Spirit. Working with trees for mental and emotional balance is impactful because trees have an energy field that is much like our own aura or energy field, and connecting with one tree brings us into connection with all of nature, which fuels our hope.

The tree has consciousness, or aliveness, and you may sense the energy of the tree. You can trust that when you connect to a tree in this ritual you will be connecting to the entire creation and the Universe, because we are all interconnected and inter-reliable, with the same life force energy that flows through all living things on Grandmother Earth.

Feeling a sense of connection will create hope
and increase courage.

We feel hopeless when we disconnect from life. Leaning in to connect with life and the living is the key to feeling hope when there are so many distractions that pull us out of connection. It is through the exercise of our free will that we make choices that create distraction and disconnection, and it takes our free will to choose to plug back into connection with life again.

CHAPTER 10: KNOW FEAR, NOT NO FEAR

"Courage starts with showing up and letting ourselves be seen."

Brené Brown

I was once driving along a remote two-lane highway at 70 mph, with a line-up of six cars driving towards me in the opposite lane. Suddenly, the fourth car from the front pulled out from the line of cars and into my lane, intending to pass the three front cars. I had no time to apply my brakes to stop and there was no room to swerve out of the way. There was a steep drop off on the right shoulder of my lane and the oncoming cars were on my left. The car heading towards me had moved to drive down the center of the highway, so there were three cars abreast on a two-lane highway. In that moment, I felt my full stress hormone response kick into survival mode to save my life, otherwise there would have been mass casualties, and I would have been one of them!

Time stopped and my vision narrowed.

Laser focused on the *gap* between the edge of the road and the car coming towards me, I took a deep breath, dropped down to my one-point (that power place in my lower belly), gripped the steering wheel tighter and leaned slightly forward as I hit the accelerator and shot through the gap.

I made it — between the edge of the road and the oncoming car! I didn't think about it. I simply responded in an instant. I missed a major head-on multi-vehicle accident, literally by inches!

Once the moment passed, I looked in my review mirror to glance at the passing cars and kept driving down the road without missing a beat, reflecting that I was grateful to be alive. I was alive because I responded to the threat by going into pure action, accessing my fully activated fight-or-flight survival response. What I accessed in that moment was courage and pure presence as time slowed down. I didn't know if I could make it through the gap without crashing, but I made the unknown *known* by keeping my laser focus on the gap and not on the car that was coming towards me at full speed.

Fear is one of the full spectrum of possible human emotions — the one that can stop us in our tracks if we allow it to trigger the fight-or-flight stress response as our default mode for every stressful situation in our day-to-day life.

> Fear will always show up when we are facing the
> unknown and can be a major stress trigger for
> anxiety or avoidance through our sabotaging or
> distracting behaviors.

In the human design, fear is triggered as an adaptive response to our desire to stay safe from physical harm, serving to help us to be alert to possible danger or threat. We are wired to feel fear when we engage in high-risk behavior. The key here is what qualifies as a high-risk behavior — is it jumping from an airplane with a parachute, standing in front of potential clients giving a presentation, preparing to have a difficult one-on-one conversation, or some other activity outside of our comfort zone that happens in our day-to-day life? The emotion of fear, and how we cope with it, can become a habit if we don't have empowering tools or strategies to meet life's large and small challenges that trigger fear.

This acronym describes fear we feel that is not associated with a true physical threat, but one that we may perceive as "threatening" behavior:

False
Expectations
Accepted as
Real

When confronted by the unknown, we may be facing something we don't have experience with that is not part of our memory, our concepts, frame of reference, or prior skills for engagement. Fear in this context is related to our insecurity, which will shake our confidence. The unknown is a confrontation to our self-concepts in terms of our self-acceptance, self-worth and self-disseverment, which opens the door to our insecurity.

Fear can also be triggered by something experienced in our past that led us to encode a painful outcome, such as being a poor test taker who freezes during exams, or someone who was bitten by a dog and now has a fear of dogs. A simple example of how fear was encoded following a bad experience happened when I tripped the security alarm at the center where I teach. The alarm was blaring, the phone was ringing, and while I was trying to push the keypad buttons to shut off the alarm, I couldn't answer the phone to prevent the police from coming. It was a chaotic, tense moment of panic.

From that one experience I encoded a fear of operating the alarm system. I went for years going to any extreme to not be the person turning the alarm on or off. I had a deep fear about the alarm because it triggered fear that I would make a mistake, trip the alarm again, and be "in trouble" with authoritative figures. I know it sounds like an episode of *I Love Lucy*! On that day, I encoded a fear from that bad experience that triggered stress and anxiety for several years, until I created a strategy to cultivate courage to encode a new relationship with the alarm keypad. I still respect the arming and disarming process with hyper-vigilance.

> Fear is considered an enemy of self, as it will
> often trigger resistance, causing us to lose our
> focus and become distracted to avoid what we
> fear. We will go to extreme measures to avoid
> something we are afraid of.

Fear can be the energy underneath our procrastination or sabotaging patterns that we enact when we are in resistance. To avoid stewing in the emotion of fear, we may numb out by any of the distractions that pull us out of the present moment, such as social media scrolling, emotional eating or having an extra alcoholic beverage or two.

If our life is truly threatened, we do want to experience the fight-or-flight response from our stress hormones so we can take action to ensure our survival. But if we always respond to our daily stressors with the fight, flight or freeze response, we will constantly submit our body to the flood of survival hormones from the sympathetic nervous system, which is exhausting and makes us vulnerable to a long list of stress-related illnesses.

Fear of the unknown may make us feel anxious, even without a true physical threat to our life. This is true if we lack confidence when we learn something new or step into change, even if it is a positive change, like starting a new job. If we lack tools or strategies to meet our perceived threat with courage, our fear may stop us from moving forward, or block us from learning something new. Fear can trigger anxiety when we focus on the future and not the reality of what is in the present moment. Taking steps to learn what we can about the unknown will dampen our fear and increase our courage.

There is another type of fear that we feel when we face the unknown, sometimes referred to as a "knock from Spirit." This may come in the form of a stretch for excellence or an opportunity that is linked to making a bigger impact in how we are living by taking a leap of faith. We may experience this knock from Spirit with a health diagnosis or major unexpected life change in the form of a "wake-up call." This is of a spiritual nature and is experienced when our Higher Self, Spirit, or God is calling us into a big opportunity to grow personally or to step into a bigger space in terms of our personal evolution. Fear of the unknown of this nature may trigger our insecurity and doubt about our capacity to successfully stretch into our true meaning and purpose, or to put ourselves out into the world in a bigger way.

In terms of a major life event or health issue, the confrontation is to completely leave behind the known and step into the unknowable.

The lower self, or that physical part of us, wants to feel safe and stay within the familiar realm and will push our resistance to prevent us from taking the leap. The Higher Self, that part of us that is of a spiritual nature, beckons us to evolve from the opportunity and magnetically pulls us into the abyss that is linked to our destiny.

Our inner dialogue from our lower self will show up as fabrication (called pretense) that will give a convincing voice to our resistance and fear as our inner critic or pretender voice:

- Am I good enough?
- Do I have the capacity to succeed?
- How am I going to fit this into my life?
- This sounds like too much…

> If we listen to this inner dialogue, it may stop
> us in our tracks just as we feel ready to take the
> leap. We hold ourselves back when our inner
> doubt and fear take command.

Our inner critic may carry us away into a future scenario based completely on fear and fantasy, or may even imagine an entire conversation to rationalize why we should not take the leap. I call this rumination "imaginary conversations," when we get caught in our stories of pain, fear, and self-pity that convince us to stay where we are, inside of what we know. When we are able to take a pause to mindfully explore the truth about our fear, or fear-induced resistance, we quieten the inner dialogue.

Called to step into a bigger space that holds the potential for personal growth, we can feel the resistance to the opportunity as we face the unknown. On one side is the devil we know, the familiar and not too exciting reality that may feel like chopping wood and carrying water. On the other side is the abyss, the deep unknown and the potential stretch into growth beckoning us to take the leap of faith. It's exciting and terrifying at the same time. In this case, accepting fear as a companion will support us to take a humble assessment of what we know and what we don't know, and what steps we can take to make the unknown known.

The Pregnant Pause practice will support us to sort out what is the fear factor of pure fantasy, called pretense, and what is the real opportunity and edge from which to grow. This is the type of stress that we want to commit to meeting as a challenge, not as a threat to our success and life.

Here we can apply what we learned in Chapter 1 about the different types of stress responses beyond the well-worn fight-or-flight response. The two alternative stress responses are how we master our stress. The stress trigger may poke at us, but we have a more productive way to meet our stress for the times we are not in danger or physically threatened.

The meet-the-challenge stress response will support us to be willing to take the plunge and learn as we go. The tend-and-befriend stress response will help us to dampen our fear and increase our courage and confidence to leap when we have the support of someone near and dear to share with about our decision process (someone we trust who we can lean into for support).

If we choose the fight-or-flight stress response, which may be our default response, we will feel anxious, stressed, and feel the effects of the stress hormones that trigger our survival instinct. This means it will take much more effort and energy to push through our own fear and resistance to gain from taking the leap into the unknown. It's like kicking and screaming through it when we could use one of the stress mastery responses and gain energy, without wiping ourselves out in the process.

Practice: The Pregnant Pause

Use this technique any time you are feeling "stuck" in your thinking or emotions from feelings of fear, resistance or insecurity of the unknown.

Write the steps down on an index card or sticky note and have it handy and visible.

This Stress Mastery practice supports you to "feel" into the reality of what is happening so you can choose how to move through it without analyzing it or ruminating about it in your inner dialogue. Take 1-3 breaths deeply into your center, to come home into your one-point.

Ask yourself these questions:

- What do I know?
- What do I not know?
- What is the truth?
- What action can I take that will empower me and not sabotage me?

Have a list of things you can do to shift your mood/thoughts/beliefs/ energy:

- Say a prayer.
- Go for a walk.
- Make a cup of tea.
- Call a friend.
- Meditate
- Speak your turnaround mantra: a short and snappy turnaround phrase that is so opposite to your inner dialogue that it makes you laugh internally to say it (see Chapter 12 for a full description).
- Take ten deep breaths into your one-point or center.

CHAPTER 11: ALLOW MISTAKES TO GAIN MASTERY OVER PERFECTION

"Experience is simply the name we give our mistakes."

Oscar Wilde

I am a person who naturally takes on leadership roles because, of course, I want to be reliable and pleasing to others, and mostly because when they ask, I say yes. Many leadership opportunities have come my way because I was the one who did not say no.

In leadership, I was often paralyzed by my self-inflicted doubt of not being good enough or skilled enough. I drank the anxiety cocktail any time I had to speak to a group or lead an event. I poured a lot of time and energy into my preparations to get it right, with a desire to appear competent and gain accolades from others. I was filled with anxiety of what others would think of me if I made a mistake or didn't do an amazing job. My greatest and most paralyzing fear that triggered my resistance was the fear that I would fail in some way. I was insecure in myself and lacked confidence, yet somehow, I always rallied to show up prepared for my roles, which felt like torture internally.

Like a self-fulfilling prophecy, my fear of making a mistake would overcome me and pull me out of presence by triggering my inner dialogue, causing me to lose my place, skip ahead and make a mistake! During my performance anxiety, my heart pounded, I shook like a leaf from head to toe, and my mouth ran so dry that my lips stuck to my teeth, making it difficult to speak. I was super-charged with the fight-or-flight stress response. Afterwards, I would dwell on my lack of perfection, listen to my inner critic, ruminate about my mistakes, and not integrate or anchor what went well from my experience. That approach is like throwing the baby out with the bathwater — focusing on what didn't go well about the event, negating any success or learning from the experience.

As I studied stress resilience factors, I discovered that what I was calling "performance anxiety" could realistically be reframed as "excitement" for the opportunity to grow personally within a continuum to get better.

> In the physiology of stress response, the body
> doesn't know if we are feeling anxious or excited
> emotionally. If we tell ourselves we are feeling
> excited, we can stay on track with the meet-
> the-challenge response to learn and grow at the
> edge from the experience.

If we label our feelings as fear or anxiety, we may tip into the fight-or-flight response, where the body perceives there is a threat or danger.

The attitude I would tell myself to get off the anxiety ledge and into the learning mode was, "I'm excited for this opportunity and I hope I do well. I know I can learn from this experience and do even better next time."

> The trick is in reframing perfection into the
> concept of mastery or excellence, where the
> experience is a *process for improvement* and not
> a bar that is too high to reach.

It's a game-changer when we embrace the concept that perfection is a finite destination, and the idea of mastery as a continuum of evolving into something better with no end point. It also helped when I was able to stop comparing myself to the false expectations of others and trust that I was working towards my personal best.

The physiology of stress is the same whether it's *good* stress or *bad* stress, and we have the choice to label it *anxiety or excitement*. It is very freeing when we can talk ourselves off the edge of the anxiety cliff by reframing how we feel as excitement, not as the freak-out related to anxiety.

> The right mindset is like secret sauce, because
> if we trigger the anxiety track we will likely
> go into the fight-or-flight response, and if we
> trigger excitement we will go into the meet-the-
> challenge response. Performance and learning
> are always better when we are in our excitement
> frame of reference. We can ask ourselves, "Am I
> anxious, or am I excited?"

Sabotaging ourselves into making mistakes from anxiety is very painful when we see how we are tripping ourselves up. Perfection will prevent us from taking action if we feel we aren't good enough or prepared enough. We miss opportunities when our lack of courage to go for the stretch keeps us stuck in our resistance. This repression energy will hold us back from actualizing our true gifts to shine.

I always said yes if I was asked to do something, but left on my own, I simply did not put my hand up to volunteer. I perceived I wasn't good enough or ready enough to meet my self-imposed standards of perfection of what I *should* do. I often compared myself to others to see if I measured up, which is a sure way to trigger insecurity. I would go into an inner battle with my resistance dialogue, while others instantly volunteered to participate. I was so envious of those who shot their hand up for an edgy opportunity with a clear intent to learn. I held myself back if I felt I wasn't masterful or skilled, particularly if it was something where I lacked expertise or experience. I lacked compassion for my learning curve. I would judge myself as good or bad, right or wrong, staying in tunnel vision and black and white thinking, rather than creative problem solving to see a new perspective.

> Perfection leads to pushing energy and is
> exhausting, while mastery allows for expansion
> as we grow into something new.

As a life lesson in self-acceptance, I finally learned how to relax into "feeling excited" and allowed the mistakes to happen while having fun at the same time. One of my mentors gave me the assignment to go to karaoke night with my "Fan Club." My assignment was to sing songs and make as many mistakes as possible. The edge was to be up front on center stage and to make mistakes on purpose. My fan club was there to support me and love me no matter what. I might mention that I did this assignment sober and learned to let go and not worry about the judgment of others. The real gift was allowing that rowdy, not-so-polished woman out of the box, laughing at myself, and seeing that being too serious was going to spoil the fun.

Whenever I start to feel the twinges of anxiety, I have a heart-to-heart with myself that I'm truly excited about the opportunity in front of me and I acknowledge that I want to do well. I remind myself that I was the one who said yes to the opportunity, and that my nervousness is all self-inflicted. Then I follow up with some of my other techniques to be present, neutral and fully at "home" in my one-point. Basically, I talk myself off the anxiety ledge and use centering practices to stay relaxed and focused.

> The secret is in how I assemble myself internally
> to settle into my womb space, hold my center
> and connect to the present moment externally.
> I prepare my inner sanctuary in advance of the
> engagement.

Now when I make mistakes on my videos or stutter in one of my talks, I embrace my freedom as I give myself permission to let go of perfection and accept the mistakes as the stamp of my authenticity. I take a pause and celebrate the times I've allowed myself to make a mistake and not go into a spin afterwards. When I'm teaching and I make a mistake, I use it to model good mistake-making skills, which inspires my students to feel more self-compassion with their own mistakes. It takes the pressure off those around me if I take the pressure off myself and hold the mantra that mistakes are part of the learning process. If a toddler is learning to walk and topples over, we don't say the baby made a mistake, we laugh and say, "How cute, the baby is learning how to walk." Therefore, accepting our mistakes as linked to our learning curve is key to gaining wisdom.

The concept of perfection comes up for many of my students and clients as a frustration and limitation. It's an act of self-acceptance and self-love to let perfection go. To start, we have to let go of any attachments or expectations to an outcome in terms of what that outcome has to look like. Conquering perfectionism also requires that we open our mind to new perspectives of realistic measures for excellence and success. The most difficult fear to shift is our attachment to how others perceive or judge us. The truth in most cases is that the only person judging us is ourselves. When we stop allowing perfection to be our key driver, we can open ourselves up to stepping onto the stress mastery path with relaxation and focus and step off the tightrope of needing to get it right.

Perfection is a limitation when it opens the door to what I call the "all or none" principle. Perfection allows for things to either be all good, or all bad, with no gray zone in between. The problem with that is that the gray area is where the learning curve sits. The thought or belief "if we don't get it right, it makes it all wrong" is a trap of limited thinking. Many of us are "all in" if we can do well, but if there is a learning curve, we will take no action at all. Through this form of black and white thinking we will not access our creativity, spontaneity, or explore our imagination to free think how we can engage to learn something new.

The shadow behind perfectionism is insecurity. The flip side of the coin of insecurity is confidence. Insecurity leads to fear and confidence leads to courage. In our insecurity we will stack our deck to ensure success. A perfectionist will excel in planning and preparation to cover every detail so we can approach the opportunity with a boost of confidence and courage. The reality of insecurity is that we may not have experience or practiced skills in the arena in which we are engaging.

> Admitting our insecurity to ourselves gives us permission to let go of perfection and allow the mistakes to happen with self-compassion so we can stay open to the learning.

There is something both freeing and humbling when we can see a truth within our shadow habits and patterns, and something empowering when we take responsibility for the not-so-shiny aspects of our persona. Once we have awareness of our inner shadow of insecurity and fear, we can take steps to battle our inner darkness, no longer ignorant of the truth of our operating system. We recognize we need a new program, a version 2.0. I would call this "shining the light into the shadow" to highlight it for examination so we can poke a stick at that pattern and explore how we can turn it around. As long as our shadow is a blind spot, we will be at the effect of it. Perfectionism is simply a symptom of our inner insecurity and fear of being exposed as not competent or not worthy.

> Remember that we cannot turn around anything until we gain the self-awareness to see it. This awareness comes as an illumination.

Once we see it, we can take responsibility for it and make a change. In taking responsibility for our own desire to change, we empower ourselves with maturity as a human "being."

Practice: Anxious or Excited?

Any time you are feeling nervous or anxious about making a mistake, or taking on an edgy new opportunity, you can ask yourself these questions:

- Am I anxious or am I excited?
- What can I gain personally from this opportunity?

You have a choice when you notice the butterflies start to flutter. You can label your feelings as excitement, since the body is unable to distinguish the difference between anxiety or excitement in the physiology of nervousness. If you know your tendency is to label your feelings as anxiety, play with what happens when you label them as excitement.

Once you choose to label your feelings as excitement, then have a heart-to-heart conversation with your Self to step off the anxiety cliff and out of the perfection box.

Create your personal agreements for the engagement with your Self:

- I'm going to allow the mistakes to happen so I can get better.
- I want to learn and grow from this experience.
- All I need is a starting place to build on so I can work towards mastery.
- I let go of any expectations of getting it right the first time.

CHAPTER 12: STRESS JUNKIES THRIVE IN CHALLENGE MODE

"There is no challenge more challenging than the challenge to improve yourself."

Anonymous

As a stress junkie, I had a huge epiphany when I saw the dark side of always engaging in challenges as my primary motivator for engagement, which made me very goal oriented. Thinking my proclivity to meet the stretch was a strength, I would push my way through to the other side of challenges to feel good about myself in terms of proving my self-worth to myself. I pushed myself to invest in my value and competence every time I successfully met a challenge.

I unconsciously opened the door to challenges for the sake of creating stressful situations, then invoked the "stress elixir" to rescue myself so I could push through, consistently saying yes to challenging "opportunities" without a filter for discernment. I never asked any questions to explore what level of commitment was required behind the door of the opportunity before I said yes. I danced in chaos to whip up more challenges to engage with. I spread myself thin in that choreography.

> At the core is the theme that we often feel
> stressed by those things we are resisting.
> Fighting our own resistance is extremely
> depleting, as we dance in the push-pull of
> saying, "Yes, I'll do it," and then internally
> saying, "No, I can't do it." Resistance will knock
> on the stress door every time.

The paradox was that my relationship with challenge was rooted in past insecurity, yet it was also the motivation to push for my success. It was my own insecurity that drove me to over-achieve and over-give my energy and time. This dance wiped out my health and immune system many times, yet I can appreciate how it worked for me then and why I need to do it differently now. It's truly humbling to see the truth of the extreme lengths I went to in my efforts to hide my insecurity from myself, and from others.

A natural leader, I was motivated from a position of external approval to hide my internal struggle to hold it together. How many people looked at me and wondered how I did all the things I committed to, like some kind of super woman? I accomplished so much, yet felt I could do better, because I was always looking at where I wobbled, rather than integrating the wins into success. I didn't celebrate my achievements and blew right past my success onto the next challenge, like a frog jumping from one lily pad to the next. In fact, I rarely acknowledged an accomplishment to anchor in joy or satisfaction for my efforts. More commonly, I would listen to the inner critic that made disempowering excuses for how I could have done better, or drill into where I did not meet the mark. I would focus on my lack, not on my personal gain.

The gap that chasing challenges created for me was that I was unable to integrate my experiences along the journey because I was too focused on the destination. But despite the lack of taking in my success as empowerment, instead dwelling on my perceived failures, there was a steady dedication and commitment to excellence that remains one of my core values of who I am.

My approach — keep pushing and striving — was exhausting. I recognize this pattern in my clients when I see that they show up on the outside as superstars and high achievers, but it is not congruent with how they truly feel about themselves on the inside. This is when I recognize the broken heartedness that blocks them from self-acceptance, self-love and true self-actualization, and overall, feeling a lack of fulfillment from the successful life they are living. One of the indicators for my lack of fulfillment was the quality of relationships that resulted from the impact of this pattern of constant doing and not prioritizing quality time to be with another. Busyness and quality time do not complement each other.

When life was stressful and chaotic, I would say, "I'm having a challenging day today." Partly because I was trying to talk myself off the edge of the anxiety cliff, but I also didn't want to sound like a complainer or have a negative tone about the overwhelm and anxiety I really felt in my challenging circumstances. I was masking the truth, even from myself, because I wanted to project an attitude that I had it all together. I used self-importance to project that I was competent and capable of meeting chaos and adversity with a "can-do" attitude. Truth is, I was pushing my way through my own resistance to meet a challenge that felt hard or complicated. It cost a lot of precious energy, and the continual flood of stress hormones wreaked havoc as I chronically triggered the fight-or-flight stress response, to the point it felt like "crack" as the juice that kept me moving forward.

I have gained much in my life through investment in my self-growth, and have been evolving as a person at a steady pace with a growth mindset. Internally, my motivation for learning and self-improvement was to "fix" myself so I could feel happy in my life and increase my self-worth. But the price from pushing and striving to get the success out of the challenge has had an impact on my joy and happiness. I have burned the candle at both ends, wiped out my health, and sabotaged my key relationships. My creativity and receptivity suffered, and I became very self-reliant, putting a lot of energy into my work, rather than delegating or asking for help. This was exhausting, but I didn't want anyone to see how hard it was for me because I wanted to be perceived as holding it all together. It was a badge of honor to do things without support, simply to prove my value to myself.

It was during a pivotal shamanic ceremony that I saw the dark side of my relationship with challenge. I'd always seen it as a strength, but I learned how my strength was also my greatest weakness. It was as if Spirit sent me an email message in all upper-case font. When the impact of truth hit me with CHALLENGE it was so LOUD in my intuitive hearing, a big wake-up call. I saw that for me, the way I engaged with challenge was a symptom of my lack of self-respect.

Once I saw the shadow within my concept of challenge, I needed to shift my perspective to see how I had created a negative relationship with the energy of challenge. It was like taking the concept of *stretch for excellence* into the energetic of *do or die*.

> Now, rather than associating the word *hard* with
> challenge, I tie the word *adventure* to challenge.
> This helps me to pick up a new perspective
> of humor and an invitation to not take life so
> seriously.

Seeing challenges as an adventure feels lighter and more joyful, with an element of fun and pleasure, accepting full responsibility for the challenge I have created, without going into blame or self-pity about my circumstances. When challenge is framed as *hard* it puts me into resistance to avoid the situation. Then I procrastinate, sabotage through distraction, and spin my wheels in stress, ensuring I will be unproductive and lose energy.

Now I'm able to truly value a new approach called Maximum Effect with Minimum Effort (aka maxi-min). Efficiency in this principle relates to how road bikes race, catching the draft from the bicycle leading the pack. It's easier to pedal when we can catch the wind draft from the bike in front of us, which is why we see the cyclists in such a tight pack in Tour de France Road bike racing.

I often find the pressure of challenge is less when I ask for support from others. I think, *"Who can help me with this?"* I look for ways to exercise my receptivity muscle, and when someone offers their support I say, "Yes please." If I can take the pressure off to not do it solo, there is freedom when others support me with their energy. This is supporting me to turn around fierce self-reliance and tap into my receptivity and creativity in working with others, and there's the added benefit of sharing the load with a friend, which fuels connection and fulfillment through co-empowerment.

Additionally, I may find a way to infuse pleasure into a project to lighten up a heavy lift when I connect the task with pleasure and fun.

Practice: Exploring My Yes

I've developed a process to discern how to say yes when opportunity knocks, and to determine if it is a realistic commitment. This five-step process supports me to take a pause and not go to my automatic yes:

1. What are my underlying values and priorities that matter to me today?
   What is most important to my personal values, and how does this opportunity align with my heart's desire — what I "want" to do versus feeling like something I "should" do?

2. What is a realistic assessment of the time investment?
   Is this a long-term or short-term commitment? Do I have the bandwidth to take this on and do it well without spreading myself too thin?

3. The principle of Maximum Effect with Minimum Effort (aka Maxi/Min Law) as the Harmonic Law of Efficiency is a Universal Law in shamanism that is key in my approach.
   What resources do I have for support so I can keep my energy tank full and not deplete myself by pushing and striving to make it happen?
   What is an efficient way to do this that is sustainable to my energy resources?
   How can I catch the "draft" energy by inviting the . contributions of others so I'm not doing all the heavy lifting.

4. What personal values compete for my time and attention with this opportunity?

   A classic example is when we really want some *me* time, and we also value family time. Both are important personal values. There may be something I really want to do (me time) that is in direct competition with another value that is also important (family time). If I choose one over the other, I am compromising. This choice may open the door to feelings of guilt or resentment. Sometimes I do compromise by choosing one over the other, and I do this with a clear awareness for the choice I make.

   More often, I ask myself how can I do both? How can I make my decision a "yes and" rather than an "either or" proposition? What contingency options can I put into place to say yes to both options so I can say "yes and...." Staying out of polarizing indecision takes a flexible and creative mindset to let go of the rigid tunnel vision that limits my ability to see other possibilities. Contingency, bump plans, and creative solutions are available when I can explore a way to honor both options, responding to the whisper of the inner, "Yes, I would love that," and tuning into my heart's desire for what I want to do versus listening to the louder, and at times critical voice, telling me what I should do.

   This approach of prioritizing our heart's desire is how we cultivate true happiness.

5. What are my bottom lines or boundaries that I need to have, or the clear agreements I need to have for myself and am able to communicate, before committing to a yes?

Today, when I'm faced with resistance, often tied to a challenge, I ask myself:

> Where is the joy factor? How do I invoke an attitude or approach that aligns with the energy of adventure, helping me to hear my inner yes so I can be in more flow, with less resistance?

I place my attention on what I have, as opposed to what I lack, so I can tune into my true happiness and gratitude in the moment.

One of the quickest ways to lighten up my negative attitude when I catch myself either pushing or resisting with a challenge is to adopt a Stress Turnaround Mantra. I can use a short and snappy humorous mantra to instantly bring an internal smile to my face and lighten up my attitude. I say these to myself in a sassy, overly sarcastic tone with humor. This approach will flood my self-pity and help me to lighten up my attitude like a reboot.

Practice: Stress Turnaround Mantra (aka Instant Attitude Adjuster)

Stress Turnaround Mantras are powerful when used consistently. I also refer to them as the "Instant Attitude Adjuster." A simple, punchy, humorous, or inspiring statement will interrupt the pattern of the internal dialogue with the same effect of defibrillator paddles applied to the chest of someone having a heart attack. It literally zaps the loop of the internal dialogue to stun the stress voice and create a pause, followed by a reboot, so you can refocus on the task at hand. When you find one that works for you, speak it often.

We can rewire our neuropathways to create
new ways of thinking and feeling that are
stress resilient. Using a stress turnaround
mantra to access the stress-resilient meet-
the-challenge mode of stress response means
we're not heading into the fight-or-flight
mode of the sympathetic stress hormonal
response.

Using an empowering mantra consistently, as a commander voice, can derail the inner negative dialogue and access the parasympathetic nervous system to produce a healthy response from your stress.

The inner dialogue is often based on pretense or "pretender voices" that distract us from the present, like a pain loop that keeps repeating to create overwhelm, anxiety and feelings of being stressed out in our day. We can get stuck there often if we don't have a strategy to turn it around. We can access our "commander voice" from our one-point, or power place. This empowering statement will support us to lighten our mood and shift our perspective to refocus and meet our current challenge.

The commander voice comes from our core and connects us to the guidance of our Higher Self to take the high road. The pretender voices come from the inner dialogue in our mental construct, and are humorously referred to as the "itty-bitty-shitty-committee." These pretender voices are what trigger the pain tapes of our inner dialogue and are false and full of pretense. If we allow them to run amok in our thoughts, we will believe they are true.

Technique

First, identify the pretender voices that loop in your head nonstop at those times you are so busy and in overwhelm.

Identifying the voice of the feedback loop is key.

Once you know the negative voice that keeps you stuck, turn it around with an empowering statement. You can use humor in the statement, such as, "Suck it up, Buttercup," and use the tone of your voice to flood the self-pity with a sassy or sarcastic attitude. You don't say these slogans or mantras using a normal tone of voice — humor is an important component for success with this technique so you can lighten up. You want to interrupt the negative pattern to reboot into a more empowering pattern.

Following are some examples. As you read the turnaround statements, try on that sassy, sarcastic, over-the-top tone to lighten up and feel the humor or victory over the darker energy. These are meant to be the jolt of sobriety to reset your focus into the present moment and to pull you out of the pain loop running in your head that pulls you out of the present moment. They work like an instant reboot.

- For a loop that says, "I'm so busy," instead say, "I'm SOOOOO productive!"
- For a loop that says, "I'm so nervous," instead say, "I'm SOOOO excited!"
- For a loop that says, "I have no time," instead say, "The time is NOW!"
  Or like the Nike ad says, "Just Do it!"

- For a loop that says, "I'm so overwhelmed," create a little song with a melody, "I go with the flow without pushing to make it happen." Or you can lean in with a prayer and say, "My faith keeps me strong!"

Use these stress turnaround mantras often by writing them on sticky notes and posting them all around you so you see them and remember to use them. Remember, they are like defibrillator paddles to reboot your inner dialogue so you can lighten up and shift your negative mood.

Adding humor to lighten up your mood will spark more neurons to wire together from different areas of the brain, so you have the benefit of multiple streams forming the new pathway when you can add feelings, senses and emotions to the experience.

It takes sixty-six to ninety days for a new pathway to be integrated into your thinking and actions. Be consistent, and create ways to remember to use these empowering statements often.

CHAPTER 13: EVOLVING FROM ORDINARY CATERPILLAR TO MAGNIFICENT BUTTERFLY

"Why fit in when you were born to stand out?"

Dr. Seuss

We gain maturity and wisdom from our experiences throughout our life process. We each have our own unique pace for self-growth. Some will crawl along into change and growth. Some take a hop and then another hop. Others jump right into the abyss of change with a leap of faith. We are either a crawler, a hopper, a jumper, or a mix of any of these modes of transformation and personal growth at different points of our lifetime.

The metaphor of the butterfly is a powerful example of growing from stress, resistance, and challenge. Butterflies are magnificent. We often notice a butterfly as it flits from flower to flower with its delicate, brightly colored wings. There is a butterfly museum in my community where you can watch an entire display of butterflies breaking free from their cocoons. It's a long process that cannot be rushed. It takes patience. The butterfly will struggle to break free from its protective cover. The struggle is what strengthens the wings so the butterfly can take flight once it breaks free. If we interfere with the progressive struggle of the butterfly by *helping* it free itself from the cocoon, the butterfly will not be able to fly and will die. The butterfly can only fly when the wings are strengthened from the struggle to meet the resistance against the cocoon to find its freedom.

> The butterfly metaphor applies to how we grow
> as humans. *How* we meet demands that life
> presents is what creates the opportunities for
> us to grow. The key is to see our past pain and
> struggle as a life teacher, providing wisdom
> to support our growth. Do not allow the old
> stories to define us, but rather to see how they
> were the journey that refined us.

When we replay the past painful stories of pity and drama over and over like a movie, they define who we are by encoding the old stories that continue to disempower us. This mythology perpetuates the story that there is something wrong with us. Then, like a sequel, we continue to focus on the pain and drama in our life and miss the moments of power where we successfully meet a challenge or learn something from which we ultimately grow.

In contrast, reflecting on our past can illuminate insights that refined our character and built inner strength and wisdom from which we grew. We can explore the lessons learned, rather than being defined by the old story that does not reflect who we are now. An example would be someone who has healed from a disease may think of themselves as a "survivor," which implies they are still living defined as someone with the disease even though they stepped into their power and gained valuable wisdom on their journey to heal. The other perspective is someone who has healed and moved forward in their life may say, "I had a disease," or, "I recovered from my illness," referring to something from their past. Someone who is still in treatment could respond, "I focus on my healing," as a vision of hope, rather than saying, "I'm suffering from this disease," which perpetuates a pain story.

Transformation from our past is possible once we shift our identity into the potential of who we want to be in terms of being healed and whole, rather than what happened to us in the past. In shamanism we call this erasing personal history or re-writing our story. Erasing personal history does not deny that the events happened, but is a re-write of the old story into one that uncovers the inner strength to empower or provide a life lesson. When we do this, the old story loses the pain trigger and feels more neutral as we see ourselves growing from the event. These are the character-refining moments that reveal a truth about our natural self. Even the most horrific life events offer a potential wake-up call, a call to action for change, transformation, or a nugget of wisdom.

The essential key here is the degree to which we can integrate life events and challenges into a catalyst for personal growth and evolution. When we have not integrated these shock points, they become the trauma points that perpetuate more wounding as we continue to live in the pain and suffering from our past that spills into our present. Significant transformation will happen to our self-worth as we shift our identity beyond victim and survivor mode to thrive at a new level of awareness. A thriver is someone who has met life challenges, integrated their experiences and grown beyond the identity of their old story by identifying what strengths they gained to overcome adversity. Think of the expression "been there, done that, got the T-shirt."

There is a level of self-acceptance when we allow past mistakes, adversity, loss, and peak emotional experiences to be integrated as life lessons for our personal growth. When these past experiences are not integrated into wisdom or otherwise seen from a new perspective, they become shock points that will still activate as pain and suffering in our present life.

We evolve throughout our lifetime through three primary arenas where we show up in life most often. How we engage in our significant relationships, our work arena and our health are key vehicles for our self-growth. *What* we do in these arenas is not as important as *how* we show up and engage with these vehicles for growth. We may not always be able to change what is happening to us in our life, or what others are doing, but we can always shift our attitude towards life events and our approach with the circumstances, people and events in our life that are beyond our control.

> We grow from our relationships as we gain both
> light and dark reflections of ourselves through
> our engagements with others. We can look
> back at those key people who were our teachers
> in terms of our significant life lessons. We
> learn from our relationships with our parents,
> siblings, grandparents, teachers, friends, lovers,
> spouses and partners.

Role models create an impact in our personal growth. Remember the key people who have influenced us both positively and negatively and been key players inside our life story. Image makers and role models will inspire us to stretch for more. Image takers and those individuals who were difficult to engage with also made a strong impact on how we developed within our persona through adversity.

How we show up in our work (and school when we were younger) is one of our primary vehicles for self-growth, where we can cultivate our gifts to shine, as well as repress our naturalness to hide our shining behind our shadow patterns and traits.

The shadow is the mask we wear to cover up our insecurity, pity or shame, for example.

As we wake up to live more consciously, we gain access to deeper personal insights and awareness. Peeling away our onion layers through self-discovery and healing, we may now see our shadow aspects that have become part of our stress patterns and coping habits. Like an ah-ha moment, it's illuminating to shine a light into our shadow aspects so we can gain a deeper understanding of how we encoded our shadow traits to cope the best way we knew how.

> We can feel self-acceptance through empathy
> and self-compassion when we understand our
> motivation behind our shadow. This is called
> healing the shadow.

Self-awareness is the first step that leads to self-appreciation, where we understand how we picked up unskilled behavior patterns as part of survival adaptability. Once we have self-awareness through self-exploration, we can feel self-compassion for the choices that we made in the past. If we are ready to grow beyond our shadow side, our willingness to explore that part of us is the first step to making a choice to create new patterns that support our expansion and growth. Nothing will change in our beliefs, thoughts, habits, or patterns until we gain awareness. It is only through self-awareness that we can access self-acceptance. To step into a new identity of our potential, we must integrate all parts of ourselves, both shining and shadow. This is what opens the door to self-compassion and self-love.

I offer my own awareness of my shadow to illustrate this. If I expose my patterns of people-pleasing, over-giving and rescuing others, I can see my shadow of co-dependence. This pattern keeps me in a mode of self-forgetting by putting others first and myself last. The repression pattern, or hiding of my shining, comes out when I don't assert myself for what I want. When I don't assert my heart's desire, I get very busy doing for others, so the pattern perpetuates itself.

Once I saw my pattern of co-dependence, I put
a bottom line or boundary in place. One of
my strategies for an empowering attitude and
approach is to only take responsibility for what
is mine to do, and to support others to focus on
what is theirs to do. I stay mindful to remember
which lane is mine and which is theirs.

Integrating the shadow was possible when I saw how I took on co-dependent patterns as a little girl, at home and in school, to be pleasing, and to feel safe by making sure everyone else was cared for. Over time, this pattern became encoded globally into all my relationships. What it taught me was how dependable I am. I can support anyone to feel comfortable in any space. It supported me to be very successful in my life, because I always said yes to everything I was asked to do, even the stretchy new opportunities. Although this is not a sustainable strategy for success, I can say that when people asked me to step up, I did. And through stepping up, I have developed strong leadership skills. By supporting others, I was able to be the mediator, to see multiple viewpoints and to accomplish a lot by keeping my focus on the big picture, while also tracking the details.

These patterns served me very well for years, until they didn't. I finally came to terms with my own empowerment to put myself forward authentically and honestly, without fear of disapproval from those who were so attuned to my dependable "good girl" attitude.

I'm not proposing that patterns of co-dependency are a good thing (there are many areas of my life where those patterns sabotaged what really mattered), but I have been able to integrate how this pattern supported me to cope with life and move forward at the same time. I now have awareness of how to not slip back into those patterns where I gave away my power to others.

> Our work is a major vehicle for self-growth. We grow from meeting the challenges of our work and from the personalities with which we work.

Our work can be a spiritual practice when we think about the amount of time and effort we put into our life working, and the many ways we have personally grown from our work. We will always have the opportunity to stretch and grow from our experiences on the job. Working in the hospital, I used to say that my job was fertile ground to implement my teachings and practices from my shamanic studies. A big chunk of life happens during working hours. If we track the changes we have made and the lessons learned over the course of our career, we can see progress from who we were at the start of working to who we are now.

> We evolve from our health as a vehicle for self-growth when we make the changes necessary to heal from our afflictions.

Any time we take responsibility for dealing with a health problem, we are engaging in change and transformation that moves us through the process of establishing new patterns, perspectives and habits by the modifications to which we commit.

I remember taking care of cardiac patients who, before their cardiac event, had an unhealthy lifestyle that contributed to their risks for poor health. Their health status had not been an important priority for them. Then, like a wake-up call, the patients found internal motivation to change through their recovery process, which led to new lifestyle patterns and choices around values and priorities. From taking no responsibility for their health choices, they evolved into someone who may be exercising, meditating, not smoking, losing weight, and eating more consciously. This is an example of a person who is now living with more conscious awareness about their lifestyle and choices than the person they were before their health crisis. As we evolve through our health we engage with care for our physical well-being. Any health affliction has the potential to be the catalyst for a global mind-body-spirit revolution once the internal motivation is awakened.

I know this mode of growth through health challenges very well. I opened the door to significant health problems over and over, which catalyzed my conscious awakening as I met each of these health problems as a teacher that taught me how to rebalance and heal myself. To meet the challenge of change, I had to keep exploring my destructive patterns and create new patterns. My particular flavor of "dis-eases" were the autoimmune types, literally me turning on myself destructively until I accepted that I did not have to keep learning from health afflictions and could find a more productive way to evolve and grow outside of my physical challenges. The turning point in my relationship with stress was when I had the epiphany that stress was going to take me out if I didn't find a new way to deal with it. This coincided with the beginning of my journey on my shamanic spiritual path.

We grow from our life experiences at home, in our community and at work. The opportunity is to not allow adversity to define who we are by living in a victim story that becomes our identity, where we get stuck in past trials and events, rather than something in our past that was a catalyst for growth. When we recapitulate a story or event from our past, the key is to look beyond the painful details and glean what it was that we gained or learned from the experience.

How did we meet the event that showed our
strength or bravery?
What is the light within the dark of that old
memory?
How can we transform our mistakes into
lessons for wisdom?

This is how we can change our personal mythology and empower ourselves to see a new perspective of how we met adversity and challenge, or stress, in our past and actually gained something from the engagement. For example, let's say we went through a horrible breakup from an unhealthy relationship. Once we get over the blame of what happened, we may be able to see what that difficult personality actually provided to us as an outcome of the relationship ending. For example, we may gain an empowering bottom line about our future engagements within relationships. If we stay in blame and anger and stew in the old story, we may miss the hidden blessing and gift of the true lesson we gained.

Stepping out of our pain story means we don't have to repeat that type of lesson. It's like making lemonade out of lemons, as the expression goes. At some level, we may take the high road and feel gratitude to the provider of that gift. You can give away the pain and take in the wisdom.

We can grow from the positive stress of changing jobs, moving or getting married, as well as meeting an adverse event. Some of our most powerful lessons come from those experiences over which we have no control, such as being laid off from our job, losing someone dear to us or some other unexpected, life-altering event.

We all experience significant life events where we feel a powerful sense of loss. It may be the loss of a job, health, of our marriage, a failure of some type, or a betrayal from a person or organization that we care about. Significant events that put us into the circle of loss in our life will open a cascade of emotions. We may feel pity, blame, shame, grief, guilt, betrayal, anger, abandonment or disappointment. If we don't integrate the loss in terms of resolving the grief or understanding the hidden lesson or gift, we can stay stuck in self-pity or in victim mentality.

This loss may define who we are if we replay this "movie scene" over and over in our mind, or repeatedly talk about it in terms of the negative impact on our life. At that point, it can become part of our mythology that we entertain ourselves with every time we ruminate about it. When a similar event happens, we bring the past pain story forward and create more pain and drama in the present situation.

> The turnaround happens when we take
> responsibility for what this event means to us,
> or what we need to do to resolve the pain and
> pity.

Letting go of blame and embracing acceptance for what happened will support integration of the peak event to gain wisdom and maturity.

The key to stress resilience is mindset.

Mindset can shift when we open our mind to change perspectives and see another point of view. Metaphorically speaking, we can shine the light into the dark and explore how to integrate what happened as a life lesson from which to grow. If we are grief stricken, it's essential to move through the stages of grief in the timing that we need. We gain wisdom and life experience through loss, and there will always be a gift or a form of rebirth that comes from a loss. Once we resolve the loss and explore the win, we can say with humor, "Been there, done that," knowing we don't have to repeat that scenario because we picked up what we needed to learn and can move forward.

Erasing personal history is a process that supports the integration of our past stories so we can view them from a neutral, non-judgmental perspective, without an emotional charge or trigger.

> **We can't change the past, but we can shift our perspective to glean it through new eyes and make different choices going forward.**

Practice: Turn 5 Painful Stories into Power Stories

Storytelling is a powerful tool to heal the past and integrate the truth of an experience. Power stories help us to glean the wisdom gained from life's past peak events through the eyes of who we are now. We have had many life lessons based on painful experiences, or infused with drama that caused wounding in our past. We can go back and take a new look at those old stories and choose to learn from pleasure and wisdom, rather than pain and drama, using our free will to tap into our imagination and creativity to expand the memory into a new perspective.

In our past, we have encoded painful memories that may become the mythology that entertains us when we bring our past pain stories into our present and future reality, to rinse and repeat the pain and drama. We cannot change the course of the event, but we can reframe the old story to create a new "back story" that is both empowering and illuminating.

Technique

Go back into your past and recapitulate five of your most painful or impactful memories from strong experiences. Find five stories that had a big impact, where you gained a victory, learned a lesson, took a stand for yourself, or experienced a confrontation or betrayal (in shamanism, five is the number representing understanding gained from the impact of the memory). You may have stories about a loss or mistake where you have yet to harvest the bigger gain of learning from the engagement.

Replay the movie memory of your old story. This time, look for the strong spirit in your former self who met the challenge and got through it successfully, in terms of how that event changed your life or offered you a new perspective of the inner strength that showed up in the engagement. You're looking for the inner hero or heroine.

Once you catch a glimpse of the new version of your past story write down a few paragraphs highlighting the new story of that feisty spirit, or that brave or wise little kid, you will uncover the resilience that was present and catch a glimpse of your natural self.

If you're having a challenge reframing a story to see the turnaround, try telling it from your older, wiser self to your younger self to catch the empowering perspective. Another approach might be how your best friend would share the story with you.

After you've recapitulated the former story to see the power in the experience, you want to give it a new title. Here again, you want to use humor or passion to flood the pity of the old story. A title can be something like "Supergirl Saves the Day," "Accessing my Superpower to Find My Way," or "The Fearless Rebel." It's important to give your story a title that inspires humor and opens your heart so a new memory is encoded from the new perspective.

**Wisdom and empowerment are encoded from
the turnaround of the new story.**

CHAPTER 14: HEAL YOUR KARMA, DANCE YOUR DHARMA

"I am not a product of my circumstances. I am a product of my decisions."

Stephen Covey

When we commit to engaging with life 180 degrees in a new way, we have an opportunity to learn from pleasure and wisdom, rather than our default way of learning through pain and repetitive pattern. A good example is the movie *Groundhog Day,* where the lead actor does the same things over and over until he finally wakes up and gets the point that he can exercise his free will muscle and make a new choice.

For many years, I kept opening the door to significant health problems as an unconscious way to prioritize my focus on myself so I could learn my life lessons and heal. Multiple times I did this, until I finally realized I didn't need to get sick to learn life lessons. Similarly, I experienced sabotaging, co-dependent relationships until I learned how to stand in my truth and communicate with open, heart-to-heart communication to create co-empowered relationships.

These were hard lessons, and I kept stepping into the same theme of pain stories until I had enough self-worth to create a bottom line that said, "No, I'm not going to learn that way anymore, and *isn't it amazing* that I have been able to heal myself through my alignment with my spiritual path that inspires personal healing."

My clients and students ask me, "What's the difference between Karma and Dharma?" This book is founded in principles for Dharmic living and makes the assumption that reincarnation cycles exist. These teachings come directly from the Sweet Medicine Sundance Path and may not resonate with all readers. As we say before every workshop, don't believe anything I say until you see if it's true for you. It's important to free think and question new concepts before you buy into them.

Simply stated in our teachings, Karmic cycles are the evolutionary cycles that we have all come through over many, many lifetimes. Karma is based on 80% pattern and 20% free will, with lessons that are often based in emotional drama and pain stories. The Karmic ego asks the question, *"What am I going to do?"* The "what" mind is reactive and will easily default to familiar patterns. Karma is a mode of learning that will bring the same lesson to an individual over and over until that person gets the lesson. Then Spirit brings the next lesson. After so many lifetimes of this "mandatory" life curriculum, we finally get to a place where we are complete with this Karma "book" of lessons. This evolutionary state of completion of the Karma cycle is now true for many of us in the collective.

After the cycles of Karma are complete, we can open our Dharma "book" as an evolutionary leap for our Soul's maturity. In Dharma there is 80% free will. The Dharmic ego asks the key question, *"How do I want to do this?"* Dharma is not easier, as it offers many more opportunities to grow. The Dharma Book doesn't have set lessons of curriculum like our Karma Book did but has blank pages that we write on as the lessons we desire to learn. How we choose to learn often pulls us into the unknown. This is what is meant by 80% free will and only 20% of lessons coming as guided from Spirit. Exercising our free will muscle is essential or we will wipe ourselves out from the stress of stepping into the bigger, more expansive space.

There is a greater demand now to live with more conscious awareness and presence, which requires a higher vibration in terms of our life force energy or chi/ki. The evolutionary state of Dharma raises the call for us to clean up the dark side of our character that is expressed through our beliefs, wounding, choices and priorities as we engage with learning from our life experiences. Dharma is in many ways an invitation to live 180 degrees differently, when we let go of old Karmic patterns and pain stories and step into the pleasure of gaining wisdom and expansion through our desire for self-growth.

Once we step into Dharma we can't go back into Karma, because Dharma is our Soul's choice. However, our former Karmic patterns from many lifetimes, as well as this one, will spill over into Dharma. Therefore, we may recognize the way we always did things before is no longer working. Dharma will push us into finding more productive patterns with greater efficiency to conserve energy. Dharma can feel chaotic as we are constantly stepping into the unknown of new opportunities to expand into, and at the same time, exploring how to find a new way to engage with change. The Dharma reality can wipe us out from stress and the speed that self-growth opportunities are presented if we don't have the tools to meet this more expansive space.

There are many changes happening on the planet currently, including weather changes, shifts in social awareness and other forms of chaos in our collective. This is an era where humanity is waking up and stepping out of Karma cycles and into Dharma cycles, and as you know, the rules of engagement for living in Dharma are totally different than living in Karma. The majority of the planet can feel that the tides are changing, but may not have the tools, practices or wisdom resources to understand how to engage with this bigger space of evolutionary awareness.

Dharma is infused with more opportunities and a higher demand to stay out of self-pity and step into more self-authority so you can take responsibility for how you live your life. Everyone needs the resource of a spiritual path or practice as a way to stay connected to the guidance of our Higher Self or higher power, in whatever way we personally find that connection for our Soul's journey.

> We may feel that connection in nature or within a spiritual community as our way to connect to something greater that is guiding our personal evolution and expansion as a person. The demand for self-responsibility encompasses how to be part of the solution on the planet in terms of care for Grandmother Earth and her children.

Dharmic living starts with taking responsibility to step into self-authority by making a personal commitment to change those areas of our lives that are not working. Where we are not successfully navigating chaos and change indicates that we need a better tactic for our stress patterns. We can pick up the *Staffs of Power*, the blueprint for Dharmic living. These Staffs of Power offer the principles that support a Dharmic attitude and approach.

When there is so much beyond our control in our personal life, as well as in the world, we can always change our attitude and approach in how we engage with self, life and others. These five principles support us to be the driver of our own bus in our life. They are like a Spiritual GPS that guide us forward to navigate dharmic living so we can successfully meet the edge of our comfort zone to gain new wisdom and master our stress.

Five Staffs of Power as your Spiritual GPS:

Emotional Staff: Emotional willingness and maturity to assume authority for your heart's desire.
This is how we commit to engaging with life to create our own happiness, rather than waiting for life to bring it to us.

> Prioritizing the small things that matter is key
> for our happiness.

Self-authority starts when we assume authority for our heart's desire, stepping out of self-pity so we can have less concern about the perceptions of others as a mode to fuel our value and worth.

When we look outside of ourselves for approval, we will not prioritize our heart's desire and will put others first. This creates "self-forgetting," so our energy is directed on pleasing others and our needs, wills and desires are not met.

Maintaining emotional balance is a key component of happiness and being in self-authority for our emotions. Using a centering breath to drop into our one-point is an example of how we can balance our emotions so we can give with emotion in open, heart-to-heart communication. Lack of this staff is the major cause of stress and depression.

Physical Staff: Physical strength and skill to take responsibility for your health.

Care for our financial, relational and physical aspects of health is essential. Our health is one of the key arenas where we can evolve and grow when we commit to changing patterns. When we are out of balance in any of our five aspects (emotional, physical, mental, spiritual, or sexual) we will lose our health. It is our responsibility to develop the skills, strength and power to take responsibility for the actions we choose to do, or not do, with self, life and others in that order. When we don't pick up this staff, we will block our economic and personal dream success. We then conclude we don't deserve abundance so we stay with what is comfortable.

There is always a mind-body-spirit connection that shows up in our health challenges. Our health afflictions can be seen as a "knock of spirit," calling us to step out of resistance and change our patterns and get back into balance. The knock will often start subtly, getting louder until we engage the "teacher" of the affliction to realign with balance and change. If we are not aware of the knock, or ignore the knock that asks us to care for our physical body, we can open the door to a health problem that may stop us in our tracks. The lack of this staff impacts us by throwing our health out of balance.

Mental Staff: Mental clarity to co-empower self, life and others to gain individuality and autonomy.

We co-empower when we have working knowledge that we choose to share, give away, and teach. The ability to have the mental sobriety, or awareness, to clean up our patterns of over-giving, micromanaging, enabling and rescuing as a means to feel our value and competence. A lack of this staff will stop us from developing a skill or learning knowledge that we require and may also make us greedy.

Co-dependence is subtle in how it creeps into our key relationships at home and at work. We take away another's individuality and autonomy when we step into rescuing and enabling. When we step in to fix someone's problem, we keep them stuck in their problem since they are missing the opportunity to learn and grow from the engagement. Co-empowerment comes from clear agreements and boundaries between self and others, as well as learning to not fix or take on other people's problems as our responsibility. When we step into another person's opportunity to meet a challenge, gain a lesson, or help them fix their problem, we are taking away their learning and growth from the engagement that would support their autonomy and individuality. In co-dependence, we have the intention of being helpful, but it gets back to the proverb that we can give a man a fish and feed him for a day. Teach a man how to fish and you feed him for a lifetime by Lao Tzu.

Spiritual Staff: Determination to stand spiritually accountable, with the knowledge that what we do has impact for the next seven generations.

This staff is only gained after the first three staffs are achieved, as they build on each other to create more freedom and happiness. This staff demands that we are spiritually determined, imaginative, and inspired, and that we stand accountable for the impact of our dream on others. How are you going for your vision? How are you growing into your destiny with meaning and purpose using your talents, skills and abilities?

> However we make our personal connection
> to Spirit, to be spiritually accountable is how
> we live our values, walk our talk, and commit
> to our self-growth and character refinement
> through our engagement with our life lessons.

As you reflect on this Spiritual Staff, ask yourself these questions:

- Are you defined by your old story that you hold onto with self-pity and blame, or are you able to harvest the wisdom you gained from your past experiences and move forward wiser and stronger?
- Are you committed to your self-growth and healing, or are you hiding your gifts through repression and not expressing your shining? When this staff is missing we lose hope.

Center Catalyst Staff: Take Your Power

Once we can hold all four staffs, there is a level of maturity as a sacred human that allows us to access our Soul's vision to accept our destiny. This staff holds our sexual soul force freedom, which is how we catalyze our life with our essence and spark of individuality to stand within our Dharma light dance, and supports us to access our destiny, whatever that entails. This staff says, "To thine own self be true," meaning we are not at the effect of other personalities and life events around us. When this staff is missing we lack harmony.

Collectively, we are all heading towards Dharma, whether we are aware of this evolutionary state or not. We may feel the energetic shift in consciousness is happening, which may be sensed as energy speeding up, or a sense of quickening, with many individuals awakening to seek a renewed connection with Spirit. In the era of polarity and change, many have taken this time to pause and become introspective to reflect on the changes in their lives, as well as to assess their values for what really matters.

There are many streams leading in the same direction towards enlightenment, or "living lighter," and we must each find our own path with heart to which we dedicate ourselves to grow. This is why I say how essential it is that we all have access to tools, practices and resources to lean into as the current climate of chaos, change and paradigm shifts moves faster on the planet. Ultimately, to live as a sacred human means we each have access to life with happiness, health, humor, hope and harmony.

Practice: 6 Tips to Practice the Staffs of Power for Dharmic Living

Attention = Power: Where my attention goes is what grows.
This mantra is a strong reminder that where we place our focus matters. If we see the cup half empty, we will see the lack and if we see the cup half full, we will see abundance. Wherever we place our focus is what will gain power and strength to manifest either beauty and blessings or pain and drama.

- If I focus on blame, shame, pity or doubt, I will bring in more negativity.
- If I allow distraction, procrastination, or resistance to gain my attention, I gain more stress.

- If I focus on what brings me joy, happiness, and a motivating vision, I will bring in more inspiration to gain what I want for my heart's desire.

Holding Your One-Point (Strong Heart)

Your one-point can be referred to your "Shamanic Root of Power." Dropping into your one-point can be useful in a number of situations such as any time you enter a new space or join a conversation. It also supports presence, neutrality, focus, and relaxation. It is where the physical womb sits for women, also called the dantian for men and women (also referred to as your strong heart, power place, core, and your center of gravity).

When you connect with your attention into this place using your breath, you are more mindfully aware, centered, and have access to creative problem solving, as this is the seat of your intuition. You can access your inner wise self, also known as your critical observer witness, when you view life from your connection to your one-point and trust your inner GPS.

Completion versus Quitting

My teacher consistently shared that one of the key principles of Dharma was to not quit. If you quit without bringing a task to completion, the Universe will provide a lesser opportunity going forward. If you bring something to completion, even if it is perceived as a failure, the Universe will provide a bigger, more expansive opportunity to engage with. He spoke often of the rules of engagement for a Dharma lifestyle pattern so we would not forget his wise words. His legacy was to provide these valuable principles for Dharmic living that I share with you.

Focus on the how and not the what by holding presence in the now

- Asking yourself "How will I do this?" keeps your focus on the solution in the present (meet-the-challenge response for creative problem solving and learning from the situation).
- Asking "What will I do?" opens the door to reactivity and resistance and pulls you out of presence and into worry of the future or rumination about the past and can trigger the fight-or-flight response, which puts you into tunnel vision and not open to learning anything except identifying a threat.

Your Life Situations and Events are Not Your Life

Your life is *how* you deal with these effectively (holding a "no self-pity" attitude and approach).

Maxi/Min Law

All of nature operates under the principle of this Universal Law, which states that energy must be expressed with efficiency through maximum effect with minimum effort.

> Yes, I've said it before, and it's important – the number one way to gain more energy is to stop losing energy.

We lose a lot of precious life force energy through stress and resistance when our life choreography does not prioritize our decisions and choices well. Our decisions, choices and priorities do not reflect the Maxi/Min Law when we are stressed and spinning our wheels in resistance, procrastination and distraction.

The difference between other animals in nature and humans is that we have free will to choose, or not choose, an efficient approach. It's our free will that opens the door to stress, but equally, we can exercise our free will to pick up our tools and practices for stress resilience. A maxi-min approach will always include a more energy conserving mode of engagement.

> Shamanism teaches that there is only tension in nature, there is no stress. Stress is a man-made phenomenon.

CHAPTER 15: PRAYING, INTENDING, AND ALCHEMY

"Whatever you can do, or dream you can,
begin it. Boldness has genius, power and magic
in it. Begin it now."

Johann Wolfgang von Goethe

My final tip for stress resilience can be woven into all the other steps. I was taught how to pray daily by my mother before I was school age. When I was in college attending nursing school, I became overwhelmed at times with my schoolwork. My mother's answer to everything was, "Did you pray to the Holy Spirit to ask for support?"

As a family, we prayed together at the dinner table. Going through years of Catholic education taught me a lot about prayer, angels, saints, and the paradox of the Holy Trinity. The Catholic way is to pray for what we need and what we want. In shamanism this is called intending. From my Catholic upbringing, I wandered into this ancient spiritual lineage that teaches alchemy and ceremony, in combination with prayer, to intend and manifest what we desire to transform in our life. This path has taught me how we evolve and grow through our mind-body-spirit connection to nature and all of creation, including the five worlds of Grandmother Earth; the mineral, plant, animal, human and spirit worlds.

> We are all interconnected, inter-reliable and
> interrelated by the same life force or creational
> energy.

The So Below includes everything that is in form and has substance here on the physical earth, and the As Above includes all that is Spirit and formless in the fifth dimension or heavens.

> There is no separation between us as individuals
> and the world around us, including God and the
> Universe, unless we choose to go into a state of
> separation via distraction, stress, or some form
> of disconnection from Life.

This is a mind-boggling concept for our linear-thinking minds, driven by time and space in this third dimension.

There is a unique spiritual language that comes with any spiritual practice or lineage. In writing this book, I often had to pause to make sure I was using common language for some of the concepts discussed. The term God is meaningful to many, but we may not relate to the picture of a man sitting on a throne up on a cloud, like the images of God we sometimes see. If the traditional religious terms don't resonate, it's important to find a term that resonates as something greater to lean into that we can have faith in, whatever that power or energy is for us. Other examples of names for God include Yahweh, Great Spirit, Wakan Tanka, Great Mystery, Great Creator, Higher Power. I often used the term Spirit in this writing to keep the concept open and relatable for individual interpretation.

"The Universe" denotes something in the unknown, beyond us, that has great power to guide our journey, like the conductor who guides the instruments playing in an orchestra. Each individual instrument provides the harmonics to create the overall melody, all blending as one song. In the context of this book, our Soul is that part of us that is immortal and knows our destiny towards enlightenment over many lifetimes and guides us how to grow and evolve during this lifetime.

Spirit is formless and has no body. Therefore, Spirit will often show up in the form of an animal to give us a teaching or a message. All animals have an energy they represent or an energetic they symbolize as part of their naturalness. Some call these animal totems or spirit guides. We saw this with the dove that appeared above Jesus as a symbol of peace, or in the case of the burning bush, as a sign from God to Moses. Sometimes Spirit shows us a meaningful symbol or message on a billboard or a T-shirt logo — it simply pops out and we notice something profound in the moment that catches our attention. The animal world has a lot to teach us about ourselves if we study its naturalness. My students and clients love learning about their animal guides. Animals never question who they are because they have consciousness with instinct. As humans, we have consciousness with awareness and the ability to make choices using our free will. We learn a lot from our choices as we exercise our free will. Once we understand how Spirit communicates with us, we can make a connection with any form of nature that catches our focus.

Remember the mantra "Attention = Power?" This applies here too as our gaze catches a moment of power within our vision during magical moments in nature such as seeing a rainbow.

I call these signs from Spirit "medicine signs," because the only way to see Spirit is when it takes a physical form, and the impact or the message we receive in that moment can be profound. In shamanism the term "medicine" refers to the natural gift of something. The term Sweet Medicine refers to all animals. If a hawk flies overhead, I would say the hawk is a Sweet Medicine sign and can reflect on the message from Spirit coming through the symbol of the hawk.

The more we are awake, aware and alert, Spirit will show itself to us in a form that we can see or relate to, often within the context of nature. This is one of the reasons that spending time in nature is so expansive, restorative, and healing to our energy, supporting us to connect back to creation so we can reconnect to our own naturalness.

In my coaching practice and my work as a teacher of shamanism, I observe that not everyone was taught how to pray or understands how to engage with prayer. Some seek a vision of their destiny and purpose and are looking for a way to heal and grow personally. Though many are seeking connection and exploring personal healing, they may not recognize that they may be called to follow a path with heart. A path with heart is the vehicle or spiritual path we choose to commit to that will support our self-growth. There are many paths we can explore to find a way that sings to us, as our path with heart, to support our healing, personal growth, and evolution as a sacred human.

A sacred human is someone who is consciously
awake and choosing to live in the light. We are
seeking our most natural and authentic self,
or our True Nature, every time we explore our
shadow to understand who we are naturally in
our shining.

Much of the self-growth we do is to discover who we are, as well as
to understand *who we are not.* So much of what we took on in our
earlier years were the choices we made to fit in, conform, and to feel
loved and liked. We are waking up in our life to see the truth of who
we are, in both our shining and our shadow, so we can consciously
make a choice how to dance our dream awake — the dream to infuse
our life with happiness, health, humor, hope, and harmony as part of
our destiny.

It is our Dharmic destiny to align with our
gifts and shining, in connection with our
meaning and purpose, as an expression of our
individuality.

The secret I will tell you about our Dharmic destiny and purpose in
life is how we are exercising our free will muscle to create our own
destiny. Our purpose and our gifts will show up when we assume
self-authority for our heart's desire and our happiness, when we take
responsibility for our health and physical world, and when we create
co-empowered relationships with self, life and others.

**We will naturally heal in mind-body-spirit when
we determine how we will evolve as a spiritual
being having a human-being experience.**

We will create an impact when we put our shining and gifts into the world as an expression of our individuality. Picking up the Staffs of Power to live by the blueprint for Dharma is how we walk forward into our destiny and purpose.

**It's not what we are doing that matters — it's
the choices we make and the steps we take that
invite transformation. We are not waiting for
our destiny to find us.**

Prayer, intention and ceremonial alchemy are all opportunities to deepen our connection to Spirit through open-hearted communication. We must each find our way to stay connected to something greater as our guiding light. For some, it may be nature. In this connection to something greater in which we have faith, we will feel hope. We can lose hope if we disconnect or distract from connection with Spirit. Many have lost hope in the world — if they only knew that it is through connection to something greater such as God, Spirit or the beauty of nature that hope is renewed. Our choice to plug into life and live in alignment with our meaning and purpose is also where our hope is renewed.

When you pray, be clear and specific in your communication by partnering with Spirit to walk your prayers and intent into your life together. Rather than praying to be rescued or saved, pray for your needs, wants and desires. For example, we can pray for clarity to see how to move forward, or for the opportunities or doors to open that can support us. This is called determining with Spirit, and as a determiner, we are willing to be accountable for whatever Spirit brings through our prayers. It can be a surprise to see how our prayers are manifested, and the expression that we are never given more than we can handle stands true.

The important principle is that the Universe will *always say yes*. Therefore, we want to be definite with the infinite and not cast out unintentional negative thoughts. We can pray with a "yes" tone of affirmation so our prayers are answered in a positive way. For example, a prayer that says, "Please don't let me fail," (negative) versus "Support me to be successful," (positive).

In truth, there is no right or wrong way to pray, as no one can tell us how to make our connection with Spirit. Trust that when our heart is open, Spirit is listening. Spirit always knows what's in our heart, even before we speak our prayer. The reason we speak our prayers is to give our prayers a voice.

Praying for what we want and need is definitely one of the strategies to create stress resilience. Leaning into something greater than ourselves will support courage and hope to meet our challenges and adversity, with help from the hormone oxytocin, the bonding hormone which acts to increase courage and dampen fear. This mode of stress resilience is how we can co-create to manifest the life we want, using the tend-and-befriend mode of stress resilience. Prayer supports us to put our attention on what we want as *Attention = Power,* or where our attention goes is what grows. Prayer can be a mindfulness practice through reflection of our intention, while dropping us out of our head and into our heart. This is how we make our connection with Spirit a bond of trust.

Below is a ceremony or ritual you can do to support connection with Spirit and to cultivate hope using nature. During my years at the hospital, I would often slip out to the campus to make a connection with a tree if I was having a rough day. I kept a little zippy bag of loose tobacco in my desk drawer for that exact purpose. Tobacco represents our connecting link to Spirit, a tradition from the Native Americans who have always valued the sacredness of the tobacco plant. When we offer tobacco to Spirit it is like a thank you for the gift that Spirit provides to us. In shamanism we often use tobacco as our part of our alchemy in ceremony.

Practice: Connect to a Tree to Rebalance and Get Off the Mental and Emotional Rollercoaster

There are many ways to work with trees in a ritual or ceremony as a way to connect with nature. Trees have an energy for both giving and determination. They grow towards the light and are rooted into the earth. Resilient to their environment, trees can take root in the crack of a rock and grow up from the edge of a cliff and are always willing to share their healing energy with us if we ask for support.

Most people feel more balanced and expanded when they are in nature. We can't always be in nature, but we can connect to the nature around us right where we are. When we work with trees, we can find the restoration of balance and interconnection to that one tree that connects us to all trees and all of nature. We can find our nature fix right in town. For example, watering our flowers and working in our yard is a little nature fix. Hearing a fountain of free-flowing water brings us to the memory of being near the running water of a stream. We bring nature inside when we have house plants or a vase of fresh flowers.

At times when we are really impacted by the people and events in our life, we may need to do more than a simple give-away. We will heal when we forgive ourselves and others and give-away our negative thoughts and feelings.

I offer this forgiveness ceremony to adapt to your own prayers. This alchemy is a simple structure for you to create your own personal connection with Spirit using the support of a tree, which enhances your connection to Spirit. Simply stated, trees give healing energy. You can do this ceremony as often as you desire.

Flowering Tree Forgiveness Ceremony
Self-forgiveness is an important step in healing your self-pity and old painful stories so you can integrate life experiences as lessons learned and feel more self-acceptance with self-compassion for the ways your shadow patterns play out. Forgiveness is a key part of stopping the mental and emotional roller coaster when you're caught by the inner critic triggering ruminations about the past. Forgiveness is also powerful when you gain awareness of your sabotaging patterns that you are ready to turn around.

Let's get started:

- Find a tree you can connect to in your yard, in the park or in nature.
- Circle around the tree three times clockwise to make your connection and ask the tree to do ceremony with you. You will hear, feel or sense intuitively if the tree is willing or not willing to work with you. Trust what you get from Spirit through the tree, and remember that Spirit answers quickly, so this ceremony does not require a lot of time in each direction.

Start in the south. Physically connect to the tree, either with your front or your back. Ask Spirit via the tree:

- What do I need to give away emotionally that is not serving me (pity, rage, fear, anger, emotionality)?
  Speak the give-away as, "*I give away* my (name the negative emotion)," using the present tense. (Be decisive, not future oriented with "I *want* to give away....")
- What do I need to forgive myself for in relation to my emotions to rebalance myself?
  Speak the give-away as, "I forgive myself for (speak it simply)," using the present tense.

Go to the west of the tree and connect to Spirit from that direction. Ask Spirit via the tree:

- What do I need to give away physically that is not serving me (i.e. pain, fatigue)?
  Speak the give-away as, "I give away my (name the negative physical aspect)," using the present tense.
- What do I need to forgive myself for physically to rebalance myself?
  Speak the give-away as, "I forgive myself for (speak it simply)," using the present tense.

Go to the north of the tree and connect to Spirit from that direction. Ask Spirit:

- What do I need to give away mentally that is not serving me (manipulation, anxiety, control, worry, stress, negative thoughts)?
  Speak the give-away as, "I give away my (name the negative mental aspect)," using the present tense.
- What do I need to forgive myself for mentally to rebalance myself?
  Speak the give-away as, "I forgive myself for (speak it simply)," using the first person and present tense.

Go to the east of the tree and connect to Spirit from that direction. Ask Spirit:

- What do I need to give away spiritually that is not serving me (disconnection, lack of trust, doubt, insecurity, fear, hopelessness)?
  Speak the give-away as, "I give away my (name the spiritual aspect)," using the present tense.
- What do I need to forgive myself for spiritually to rebalance myself?
  Speak the give-away as, "I forgive myself for (speak it simply)," using the present tense.
- What do I commit to do to strengthen my connection to Spirit?
  Speak your commitment as, "I commit to (speak it simply)," using the present tense.

While you are in the east, say a vow or prayer to yourself about how you will commit to your journey of transformation, how you will make a commitment to invest in yourself, and how you will learn to love and accept yourself and speak whatever prayer is in your heart for your healing journey.

Thank the tree when you are complete. You can offer some of your essence back to the tree, such as saliva or a strand of hair. You can also offer the tree a gift of loose tobacco in any form as a symbol of your connection to spirit.

CHAPTER 16: GETTING TO THE DEEP ROOT OF STRESS

---

*"You can't go back and change the beginning,
but you can start where you are and change
the ending."*

C. S. Lewis

I only recently understood where the root of my insecurity, as the driving force behind my addiction to stress as a stress junkie, originated. I had never identified that insecurity was the shadow behind my stress patterns until I became aware that often I did not feel emotionally safe. Once I saw how my individuality had been attacked through teasing, sarcasm, and rage-filled authority figures yelling at me (teacher, babysitter, friend's parent, my parent) I was able to connect the dots and see how my wounding informed my identity.

I was traumatized most when I tried to speak up for my desire, share my opinion, speak my truth or express my desire to feel included. Part of growing up in my family as the youngest was being the target of teasing and tormenting from the older siblings and their friends. As for adults, there were times when their stuff came up and they let go on an innocent, or not so innocent, child. It doesn't really matter who did what. What does matter is there is a story that I have accepted about my individuality — that it was not safe for me to be authentic and express my natural ways.

I unconsciously chose to go "under cover" so no one would see who I was in my true nature or criticize me for what I didn't know or didn't do well. I would study extra hard so they wouldn't call me stupid. I took my lunch to school to avoid eating the high caloric cafeteria meals so they couldn't tease me for being chunky or fat — all the innocently spoken words that were intended to poke at me for the sheer pleasure of witnessing my torment, as kids do to each other. Their poking fun at me was never intended to wound me or become part of the story I kept retelling to myself until I believed those childhood myths. My insecurity led to my patterns of co-dependency related to over-giving, enabling and rescuing that were deeply rooted in my behaviors so I could feel loved and liked by all.

Today, I'm very aware in those moments when I'm feeling insecure. I can name it and claim it, with a tone of self-compassion. There is something very liberating when I empower myself with the truth of owning my feelings, without trying to stuff them down or hide them from others. Rather than sabotaging myself, I can choose to simply be in my vulnerability with self-acceptance. This new attitude and approach is a game-changer in all arenas in my life.

There are no two stories alike. If you turned into a stress junkie, there is probably an underlying story that wounded the full expression of your individuality too. Somewhere, there is a story that led you to hide your authentic self, laying the foundation of pushing yourself to look good and do well so your true self could stay hidden and safe until you forgot who you really are. It's what you did to protect your inner child, to keep her or him safe from the outside world. It was a matter of survival. Survival instinct is what turned on the fight-or-flight stress response, which became hardwired until you became a stress junkie with an encoded response triggered by insecurity, a lack of confidence, and fear.

My teacher, Thunder Strikes, always spoke about "individual autonomous freedom." It sounded like a good thing, but I never really understood what he was taking a stand for. Once you heal your self-concepts and embrace your individuality, you will see who you truly are in your natural talents, skills and abilities. From this point of self-awareness, you can pick up self-acceptance, self-worth, self-love and self-actualization so you can shine with your individuality fully expressed, without apologies, out into the world.

The freedom comes as you step into your autonomy, to stand in your own circle of empowerment to express your True Nature, and to transmute all self-pity into no-pity and benevolent compassion towards self, life, and others - in that order. This is what he meant by individual autonomous freedom, which is only accessed as we heal our old story that is informing a false identity and hiding our True Nature.

> The deepest layer of your stress is experienced
> when you know you are caught between hiding
> your natural self and allowing yourself to
> step into bigger spaces where you can let your
> naturalness shine.
> You know you have healed your broken heart
> when you can follow your heart's desire and
> take responsibility for your happiness.

That's my story, what is yours? Go ahead, explore your past, poke a stick at it. Shine a light to explore those old stories so you can see the light within the dark, as well as the light within the light. That's where the real healing is. Once you can see within yourself clearly, you can integrate your past peak experiences into wisdom you can grow with, then you can adopt a "no-pity" attitude of "been there, done that, got the T-shirt" with self-acceptance. This is how you heal your heart so you can feel more happiness, health, humor, hope and harmony.

The Sundance Vow

Great Spirit, I vow from this time on
to dance towards enlightenment.
I will fight my inner darkness
with any tools and knowledge that work.
I accept all teachers, teachings and paths as equal.
I honor all Paths to the Light.
I choose the Sweet Medicine SunDance way
as my Path with Heart
and the pursuit of knowledge and pleasure
as my way of self-growth.
I will learn to walk in balance with Grandmother Earth
and in harmony with her children.
As a warrior, I will fight the enemies of ignorance, superstition,
dogma, prejudice, racism, slavery, poverty,
sickness, disease, illness and death.
I vow to always honor the elders and the women
and to protect the children.
I will use my love, my physical abilities, my knowledge,
and the medicine tools in this battle with darkness.
I will empower all humans on their search
for individual, autonomous freedom.
Great Spirit, hear my intent.

Sweet Medicine Sundance Path

ABOUT THE AUTHOR

*Sara Regester, Registered Nurse, Stress Mastery
Expert, International Teacher of Shamanism
and Duke-trained Nationally Board-Certified
Health and Wellness Coach.*

Sara Regester, founder of Directions 4 Wellness, an international health and lifestyle consulting practice, is recognized as a Subject Matter Expert and supports the VA Whole Health Education Programs nationally.

After many years of witnessing the mind-body-spirit healing journey of her hospital patients, Sara saw the connection between stress and physical healing in her personal life too. Through her studies in shamanism, Sara began to understand how healing is an evolutionary process for the Spirit and Soul, not simply the physical body. Sara apprenticed to the Sweet Medicine SunDance Path in 2003, a shamanic lodge of ceremonial medicine, and teaches shamanism internationally and guides others to integrate the ancient teachings for self-growth through expansive ceremonial experiences.

Sara's expertise lies in exposing the underlying patterns that keep us stuck in our stress, sabotaging our health, success, and relationships. Sara is the creator of Stress Mastery Programs for individuals and groups, applying ancient shamanic wisdom at the heart of her deeply transformational work. Unique mind-body-spirit techniques and tools for resilience are embedded into her programs for a holistic approach to rewiring mindset and lifestyle, empowering self-healing to create a more Dharmic approach for health and happiness.

Visit www.Directions4Wellness.com for a free download of the eBook *How to Grow from Your Stress*.

ACKNOWLEDGMENTS

The concepts of this book are derived from teachings from the following resources:

Reagan, Harley SwiftDeer. 1980. *Shamanic Wheels and Keys: The Teachings of the Twisted Hairs Elders of Turtle Island Volume I.* Scottsdale, Arizona: Deer Tribe Metis Medicine Society.

Barner Ph.D., Claudia, advised by Thunder Strikes. 2000. *The Thirty Sacred Laws: The Universal and Cosmic Laws (Blue Manual Part 1). Volume II, the Teachings of the Twisted Hair Elders of Turtle Island.* Scottsdale, Arizona: Deer Tribe Metis Medicine Society.

Barner Ph.D., Claudia, advised by Thunder Strikes. 2002. *The Thirty Sacred Laws: The Magickal Laws (Blue Manual Part 2). Volume II, the Teachings of the Twisted Hair Elders of Turtle Island.* Scottsdale, Arizona: Deer Tribe Metis Medicine Society.

The Stress Mastery Programs I created in my coaching programs and the stress resilience concepts in this book are inspired by the work of Kelly McGonigal, Ph.D.

McGonigal, Kelly, Ph.D. 2015. *The Upside of Stress: Why Stress is Good for You, and How to Get Good at It.* Broadway, New York: Penguin Random House.

BIBLIOGRAPHY

AZ Quotes. "Quotes. Authors. M. Mother Teresa." Accessed March 29, 2023. https://www.azquotes.com/quote/512223

Brainy Quote. "Michael Jordan Quotes." Accessed March 27, 2023. https://www.brainyquote.com/quotes/michael_jordan_167380

Brainy Quote. "Oscar Wilde Quotes." Accessed March 29, 2023. https://www.brainyquote.com/quotes/oscar_wilde_105029

Brainy Quote. "Steven Covey Quotes." Accessed March 28, 2023. https://www.brainyquote.com/quotes/stephen_covey_133504

Chopra, Deepak. 2014. Accessed March 28, 2023. https://twitter.com/DeepakChopra/status/528335137084538880?lang=en

Good Reads. "C. S. Lewis. Quotes. Quotable Quote." Accessed March 29, 2023. https://www.goodreads.com/quotes/10348517-you-can-t-go-back-and-change-the-beginning-but-you

Good Reads. "Dr Seuss. Quotes. Quotable Quote." Accessed March 29, 2023. https://www.goodreads.com/quotes/187115-why-fit-in-when-you-were-born-to-stand-out

Good Reads. "Goethe. Find Quotes." Accessed
March 29, 2023. https://www.goodreads.com/quotes/
search?q=commitment%2C+goethe

Good Reads. "Jon Kabat-Zinn. Quotes. Quotable Quote." Accessed
January 26, 2023. https://www.goodreads.com/quotes/331826-you-
can-t-stop-the-waves-but-you-can-learn-to

Good Reads. "Margaret Thatcher. Quotes. Quotable Quote."
Accessed March 27, 2023. https://www.goodreads.com/
quotes/792731-watch-your-thoughts-for-they-will-become-actions-
watch-your

Good Reads. "Viktor E. Frankl. Quotes. Quotable Quote." Accessed
March 27, 2023. https://www.goodreads.com/quotes/52939-when-
we-are-no-longer-able-to-change-a-situation

Kabat-Zinn, Jon. 1990. *Full Catastrophe Living.* London: Piatkus.
Little, Brown Book Group.

Keller A, Litzelman K, Wisk LE, Maddox T, Cheng ER, Creswell
PD, Witt WP. 2012. "Does the perception that stress affects
health matter? The association with health and mortality." *Health
Psychology.* 2012 Sep;31(5):677-84. doi: 10.1037/a0026743. Epub
2011 Dec 26. PMID: 22201278; PMCID: PMC3374921.

Quotefancy. "Alan Cohen Quotes." Accessed March 28, 2023. https://
quotefancy.com/quote/1718866/Alan-Cohen-Everything-will-
change-when-your-desire-to-move-on-exceeds-your-desire-to-hold

www.ingramcontent.com/pod-product-compliance
Lightning Source LLC
Chambersburg PA
CBHW031504120626
46545CB00005B/1738